Group Tutoring for the Form Teacher

1 Lower Secondary School: Years One and

Group Tutoring for the Form Teacher

Group Tutoring for the Form Teacher

A developmental model

1 Lower Secondary School
Years One and Two

Programmes and Working Papers

Leslie Button

HODDER AND STOUGHTON
LONDON   SYDNEY   AUCKLAND   TORONTO

British Library Cataloguing in Publication Data

Button, Leslie
   Group tutoring for the form teacher
   1: Lower secondary school: years one and two
   1. High school teaching – England
   I. Title
   373.11′0442   LB1607

ISBN 0 340 26691 0

First published 1981

Printed and bound in Great Britain for
Hodder and Stoughton Educational,
a division of Hodder and Stoughton Ltd,
Mill Road, Dunton Green, Sevenoaks, Kent,
by J. W. Arrowsmith Ltd, Bristol.

Typeset by
Macmillan India Ltd., Bangalore

Contents

1 Working Through Groups

The Role of the Form Teacher

It has long been a tradition of British education that the school should be concerned with the all-round development of young people, and much of this has been implicit rather than explicit in the school programme. The acceleration of change in society, the growing depersonalisation of life, and changes in the school itself, have caused considerable doubt about the adequacy of this hidden approach to personal development. Something more explicit and effective is being sought. Changing technology has even entered the very fabric of established relationships – as illustrated by the revolution in sexual relationships and marriage caused by secure methods of birth control – increasing the need for explicit attention to the social and emotional development of young people.

So personal concern for young people, the nurturing of social skills and responsible attitudes, and education in personal relationships have been increasingly accepted as an important part of the school programme. Moreover, the increasing size of the school has added urgency to the need for deliberate approaches aimed at gaining a sense of belonging and commitment both to the school and to fellow pupils. The response to this has varied from school to school, but in general there has been a new urgency in the attention given to the pastoral system.

However that system is organised, the key person will be the form teacher. It is he or she who is in daily contact with the young people, and bears responsibility for creating a spirit of caring within the form. He or she will need a clear programme of work. It is not enough to offer a series of topics, since relationships and responsible attitudes need to be experienced and practised rather than to be talked about. The experience reaching the young people arises largely from the approaches used; indeed, in this context, the approach is an important part of the content. A majority of the teachers in any school are called upon to assume the role of form teacher, but the skills and approaches required may not be part of their normal experience. The insecurity of many teachers, when faced by this role, has been one of the chief obstacles to an effective expansion of the work, and it is this sense of insecurity that these programmes, together with related training programmes, are intended to remedy.

This book has been made possible by an action research project funded by the Leverhulme Trust Fund and the Health Education Council. The approaches and programmes have been applied and tested in a great variety of schools in many parts of Britain and Ireland, and in several other countries as well, and I should like to pay tribute to the very large number of teachers who have collaborated with me in developing this work. In applying and testing the materials and methods in their daily work in school, they were prepared to accept approaches that were new to them. They all committed themselves to serious programmes of training, not only for work with young people, but also so that they would be able to help, guide and support their colleagues as the work spread through the school. The use of 'we' in this text reflects the collaborative nature of the work, and refers especially to the many people who have co-operated with me in the development of these programmes.

Our experience together underlines the importance of the preparation, training and support that is required in order to adopt a more sophisticated approach to the form teacher's role. There is always a danger, when publishing programmes of this kind, that they may be seen as something ready made, that can be used didactically and apart from the approaches upon which they are based. I would like to emphasise that the methodologies upon which these programmes are based are as important as the topics and materials included within them.

There is sequence and continuity in these programmes, which facilitates the steady build-up of personal growth and expertise in the young people. The programmes are therefore offered as a coherent whole: they are not a series of exercises that can be picked out at will. This is not to say that the programme falls if it cannot be used as a whole, but anyone who finds it necessary to prune the programme will wish to bear in mind the sequence and continuity, and the inter-relationships between the topics, when making a selection. The programmes also offer plenty of opportunities for schools to add their own individual points of emphasis.

The Approach

The approaches in these programmes, which I have called developmental group work, were evolved through previous programmes of action research and experiment, in which I was supported by teams of teachers, social workers and youth workers.[1]

To be human is to be in relationship with other people. And in order to learn how to develop and maintain those relationships, a group of people must be available as an arena in which they can be learnt and practised. Developmental group work is a way of offering people opportunities for vital experiences with other people, through the membership of supportive groups who are learning to help one another in personal ways. It is developmental and educative as distinct from problem or crisis-based. Our ambition is to help young people to build up their personal resource so that they can cope more adequately with life – and its problems – as it comes along.

Developmental group work is different from counselling, which relies mainly on the one-to-one relationship between the counsellor and the young person. There will always be a need for individual counselling in our pastoral work, but the counsellor-child relationship touches only a small part of the learning experience. For example, peer relationships, especially the equal cut and thrust of friendship, need to be learnt in their own right. There is reason to believe that peer friendships are, for most people, at the core of healthy social growth, and many young people who are at odds with their peers seem to be in difficulties in many other aspects of life. As adults, we may even postpone the development of certain young people in difficulties with friendships and other peer relationships by offering our own relationship as a substitute.

The support group can operate also as a platform from which to venture into other spheres of life. It can form an arena in which the young person can learn to cope with strangers, to engage in positive communication with adults, to manage his or her own authority feelings, and to make an increasingly creative contribution to family life. In the school context, the supportive group can contribute to each member's confidence in study and participation in the affairs of the school. It can also serve as a vehicle for imparting vital knowledge about health and hygiene, citizenship, the world of work and life in general.

Personal education of this kind cannot be left to chance. It is not realistic to expect that individual need for developmental experience can be produced in a succession of lessons designed primarily for some other purpose. Time must be committed to personal education, and this is probably best attempted by the form tutor in the pastoral setting. Each young person must be encouraged to venture according to his own stage of development. The form tutor has the task of trying to be aware of the differing needs of twenty-five to thirty young people. In some schools the year head, with special responsibility for pastoral work, is expected to do this for a whole year of, say, two hundred young people. That is quite impossible. The role of the year head should be to support the form tutors and to serve as a team leader.

Time is vital. These programmes are designed for a commitment of not less than one period each week of thirty-five minutes, plus several other occasions during the week such as extended registration periods. There is enough material to fill an hour's period each week. So much depends upon the personal development of the young people that adequate time should be devoted to it; and the beneficial influence on the remainder of school life can be so great as to claim a high priority for pastoral time.

[1] For a fuller description of the models of work, see BUTTON, LESLIE (1974) *Developmental Group Work with Adolescents*. London: Hodder and Stoughton.

The Programmes

Main Themes

There are a number of main themes running through the programmes for the five years. The themes are picked up with differing intensity as the programme proceeds, according to the age and development of the young people. The effort to be devoted to the themes can be seen from the schedules which proceed the programmes for each half term. The main themes are as follows.

The Pupil's Place in the School There is an emphasis on a responsible contribution to and an active participation in the affairs of the school. It is important that pupils of all ages should feel involved, but the way in which this involvement is expressed needs to correspond to the age of the young people.

The Pastoral Group as a Small Caring Community This is the basis upon which everything else is built. Support also involves challenges: support must not be confused with cosiness. The group needs to work out its own caring programme, and the tutor will need to help the young people to establish the style in which this is approached.

Relationships, the Self and Social Skills Although this heading covers a very large area of concern, these elements are put together since they are so interdependent. The term 'relationships' is wide-ranging, including friendship, other peers, family, other adults and people in authority. The development of social skills and self-knowledge is approached with increasing sophistication as the experience of the young people grows.

Communication Skills Very rapid progress can be made here. Being articulate includes being able to identify the internal concerns and issues that are waiting to be expressed. The skill of active listening and an interest in the other person underlies so much in life.

School Work and Study Skills Which are the areas of skill and concern that are common to all school work, and can reasonably be dealt with within the pastoral programme? This section is especially concerned with attitudes, anxieties and objectives, and with group support in moving towards those objectives.

Academic Guidance and Careers Education This is an attempt to help young people to know themselves and to move towards wise decisions. It is not about ready-made advice: the initiative should be in the hands of the young people. The discussion of careers should be very much an educational programme about the world of work and other people's lives, and not narrowly about the job that the young people may take up.

Health and Hygiene Much of the total programme can be regarded as 'Health Education'; this section is more especially about health and hygiene. In most secondary schools some of the information included in subject areas contributes to health education, and it is important that there should be some co-ordination of effort in this respect.

Personal Interests This is about pursuits and leisure interests that young people can follow outside school, especially those that can be continued after leaving school. Here also there will be a need for liaison with other departments in the school.

Development of the Themes

Cyclical Treatment Each theme has its own importance at every stage of development through the secondary school. For example, friendship is a vital experience at every age, and the programme must return to the topic each year. However, it is important that the treatment should be cyclical rather than circular, so that the topic is treated with growing sophistication year by year. This has been carefully built into the five year secondary school programmes. The tutor may feel it necessary to go further than is suggested in any single year's programme because of the needs or demands of the young people, but unless there is a definite need for this, it is advisable not to pre-empt material appropriate to a later stage of the programme.

Inter-play of Themes Most programme items serve more than one purpose, or serve to bring together several themes that are running in parallel. For example, the communication skills programme includes the preparation of agendas and enquiries, and this skill is used, for example, in an enquiry addressed to parents which is also about child-parent understanding. This in turn leads ultimately to the young people preparing for their own parents' evening, which will proceed in part through a discussion of the public statements that the young people have learnt to make. Similarly, the young person's growing skill in self-assessment serves both his personal development and his progress in school work.

Sustained Continuity Threads are developed from week to week, from term to term and from year to year. To focus on only one example of this: the development of conversation skills involves the formulation of frameworks and agendas, which begins on the very first day. These skills are used in the preparation of enquiries, which lead to report sessions involving public statements to the whole group. In the second year, these skills in formulating frameworks and agendas are taken further and used more formally for year meetings and other forms of public statements. By the middle of the second year the skill of formulating frameworks is reversed in the practice of note taking, which is immediately used in receiving visitors to talk, for example, about health and hygiene. All these skills will be used extensively in the third year subject choices and careers education programme, and will finally play an important part in revision techniques and preparing for examinations.

Using the Programmes

The programmes are outlines and not straitjackets, and are designed to make room for the school's own special interests and emphases. They are planned on the assumption that young people moving into the second year will have had experience of the first year's programme, and if this were not so, it would be advisable to include some of the introductory work from the first year when introducing the programme to young people in the second year.

The first-year programme is planned on the assumption that some priority will be given to an induction and settling-in programme. It is suggested that the first day in its entirety should be devoted to the induction programme, which should continue for a single period each day for the rest of the first week. This is indicated in the planning schedules which precede the first eight stages. The remainder of the programmes are laid out in half term blocks. An outline of each half-term programme is given, followed by a detailed programme for each stage, which will approximate to a week's work.

The programmes are supported by working papers, some of which are intended as notes for the teacher, and others are to be used by the young people. It is permissible to duplicate the papers required for use by the young people. It is important that each young person should establish a file of completed working papers. Some of the continuity of the programme depends upon reference back to previous statements and some of the papers include a statement of objectives to which later reference will be made.

2 Some Basic Skills and Concepts

The Tutorial Group as a Caring Community

It is vital that the tutorial group should be established quickly as a home base, as a small caring community, and the tutor will need to lead in this direction quite deliberately. The natural situations that grow up amongst young people may not be supportive at all. Small knots may support one another, but the general situation within a total group can be divisive to the point of destructiveness. Any likelihood of ridicule will prevent risk-taking, and this will affect academic work just as much as the pastoral programme.

The ease and warmth of the group, or its prickliness and coolness, will depend to some extent upon whether members of the group have made contact with one another personally, and it is important that the group members should come to know one another as rapidly as possible. To this end, we normally encourage both verbal and physical contact by taking one another's hands with a few words of introduction. You will notice that I use the term 'hand-taking' and not 'hand-shaking'. The hand-shake can be perfunctory and conventional; we use hand-taking as a symbolism, as an initiation of a rather special situation where we are learning to support and care for one another.

Taking hands is sometimes resisted by certain groups of young people. It is not just a matter of the young people individually finding it difficult: it is sometimes seen as not permissible in front of peers. The resistance may be strong enough to make the tutor question the advisability of persisting with this part of the work. It may be important to explain the purpose of hand-taking as a symbol that marks the beginning of a new kind of activity. Some discussion about how this change of atmosphere and purpose can be achieved often helps. Contact between boys and girls is sometimes especially difficult. With a little persistance we are usually able to break through, and the meeting and greeting contributes something very important to the whole programme. There is a strong inter-play between this and, for example, receiving visitors and a number of approaches to the development of social skills. The initial steps can be helped by having several other adults with the tutor, or a few older students who have had this kind of experience.

Part of the symbolism represented by hand-taking is that we are *making contracts* with one another for mutual support in the pastoral group. Making contracts is a vital concept. Once that is well established, brief reference in any subsequent step may be all that is necessary. When first establishing the concept, it is usually worth devoting a little time to small group discussion about what is meant by making contracts. At the outset, there will only be the most general ideas about supporting one another and about participating in the group's activities, but as the programme progresses, it will be about group and mutual support for individuals undertaking personal exploration, and attempting to try new approaches to life. For this reason, contracts need to be made and remade – at the early stages it is not possible for the young people to perceive the personal movement open to them, and the need for support that may arise later.

Caring and Administration

It is vital that the young people should come to see the pastoral group as *their* group, and the tutor will wish to seize every opportunity of bringing them into the centre of decision and responsibility. This means that the young people will need to take a major responsibility for ensuring that any of their group who are in difficulties receive the support that they need. The approach to this may need to be formalised and structured into the programme.

It is suggested that the tutorial group should appoint a small caring group, who will make sure that individual members of the group are cared for. They will see that the group as a whole does not overlook absences, illness, accidents, bereavement, or any other personal difficulties.

The young people should be concerned that the members of their group are at school, and that would include looking at absenteeism and truancy. It is not intended that the caring group should provide all the support, but rather that they should alert the group as a whole, and make sure that the need for action is not overlooked. This is a responsibility that can be shared around, by reconstituting the group every term or half term.

There is usually a good deal to be accomplished by the tutor in pastoral time, and teachers sometimes complain that routine administration can run away with the time. The tutor will need to look carefully at the administration that has to be accomplished, to identify those parts that demand his personal attention, and the other routine chores that would be within the competence of a small group of young people who were trained to accomplish them. It is suggested in the second year pastoral programme that an administration group should be appointed with this in mind. Here again, the membership of the group would change regularly, so that this kind of responsibility and experience is shared as widely as possible.

Focus on Support

With a supportive situation we can achieve a great deal. The timid youngster is much more likely to venture if he feels that the situation is safe, and that he need not fear ridicule or rejection. Greetings, hand-taking and making contracts are all part of building up a supportive situation.

The tutor's style of leadership is vital here, and he will need deliberately to lead support. He will do this by tone of voice, gesture and the general atmosphere created. But it will also be necessary to focus deliberately on supportive action. For example, 'Hold it a moment! Now, let us make sure that we are supporting Tom by what we are telling him and not getting at him.' Thus the whole tone of an exchange may change immediately. We may equally need to help individuals to listen, and not to reject and thus create hostility. For example, 'Tom, are you really listening to what the others are saying to you? They are trying to be helpful.' But this can only be effective when abstract concepts like support, trust and listening are understood and felt, which is the reason that there is urgency in establishing a self-conscious supportive situation.

There can be a lot of challenge within supportive situations, as long as the challenge and criticism can be felt as being for our benefit and is not intended to reduce us. In order that someone can change his (or her) behaviour – for example, when he is earning rejection by his own behaviour – someone must *be kind enough* to help him see how he is behaving inappropriately, and usually this best comes from his peers. Generally, nothing new is being said, because the person concerned is being informed about this daily, even hourly, but usually in a hurtful, derogatory way. He is almost bound to reject statements presented in this way. The impact of a supportive situation is that the same things may be said, but the tone is different, and the person concerned is able, as it were, to cross the floor and look at what is being said with a new objectivity.

Support Exercises

Support exercises are used to present abstract ideas in a concrete way, and to help people to focus on their ability to give and receive support. Here are some examples.

The Trust Walk This is a commonly-used way of focusing on trust, support, concern and caring. The young people are asked to find a partner. One of the pair is 'blind' and the other will lead his or her partner around the room. This exercise, like so much in these programmes, needs to be carefully 'produced' by the tutor. Set the exercise going with only the basic instructions required for its initiation, and after it has been running for a few minutes, interrupt the exercise so that the experience can be deepened. Some groups or individuals may have great difficulty in taking an exercise of this kind seriously, and will fool about to cover their embarrassment. The tutor will be trying to set the tone, and voice, pace and gesture are part of this. He or she may ask at this stage, 'Are we really caring for our partners? Are we making sure that they feel that they can trust us? Now, we are really going to make our partner feel safe and cared for.' And the tutor will set the exercise going again.

There is a lot more to be accomplished yet, but we would be unwise to try to cover too much in a single step. After a little more time we will stop the exercise again and break in with a few questions. Of those who are being led we might ask: 'Has your partner managed to make you feel safe? Do you feel his concern for you? And are you able to give him your trust?' (It is important also to focus on the ability to trust other people, which some people find very difficult.)

Then we will want to deepen the experience. 'Now, what kind of experience are we making this for our blind partner? Are we helping him to meet other people? What about all the exciting things to touch and feel in the room – the different textures and temperatures?' The tutor will illustrate this by touching several things with different tactile qualities. 'Now let us begin again and make this a really important experience for our partners.' During the exercise, the tutor will move around, offer encouragement and serve as part of the experience. Before long, the tutor will move from couple to couple asking, 'Have you changed over?' and partners will change roles. If the circumstances are right, it will only be necessary to open the door and the world outside the room will become part of the experience. This might include stairs, outside temperatures, plants and flowers. Conclude the exercise with some discussion about the experience, probably in small groups with open exchanges. At every stage the tutor will be conscious of the importance of focusing on the concepts, of trust – being trustworthy and being able to trust – caring, concern and making a real contribution to the experience of another person.

Once established, the exercise can be varied and extended. It is a valuable exercise, but if it is used several times it will need to be varied in order to avoid becoming repetitive. Young people can be invited to be inventive, and they usually produce novel ways of carrying through the experience. For example, a number of groups of young people have conducted the exercise to a background of appropriate music. It is not always possible at the outset to persuade young people to conduct this exercise in mixed pairs, but this can represent a very useful extension of the exercise when leading into a consideration of boy-girl relationships.

Rocking Working in pairs, one stands behind the other, and with hands on his or her partner's shoulders, the one behind takes the weight and gently rocks him or her backwards and forwards. After a time they change places. This is about trust and caring. Some people find it difficult to put themselves in the hands of the person supporting them, and the tutor will need to encourage them gradually to give themselves to the exercise. The atmosphere should be calm and relaxed, and the tutor will need to lead in this direction by the way he produces the exercise. As a development of this exercise, work in threes, with the person in the middle being rocked forward and backward by the two outside members of the trio.

Setting the Scene

Accommodation

It will be seen from the exercises suggested above that flexibility and movement is required for this programme. We may be required to conduct tutorial sessions in a classroom too full of furniture – and not very easily adaptable furniture at that – with other school activities pressing upon us on every side. We cannot afford to be defeated by accommodation and furniture. Most classroom furniture can be re-arranged, and the interest and inventiveness of the young people can be enlisted in creating the right setting for the work. Most groups of young people quite quickly come to a point of pride in how rapidly they can set out the room. Some groups have gone so far as to time themselves with a stop watch to see just how quickly they can re-arrange their room.

When we conduct discussions we must have small groups facing one another, and if it is not possible to clear desks, we may even need to sit on them. Sometimes, conditions are so cramped that it is quite impossible to engage all the twenty-five to thirty young people in some of the exercises suggested. Then it may be necessary to divide the group into two, so that some will be participants and some observers, and then they will change over. It can add an interesting dimension if the observers are helped to establish an observation brief so that their comments can contribute to the experience.

Expectations

Expectations can be even more limiting. If this work is being introduced into a school for the first time, it may be necessary to cope with the pressure of expectations about what is and is not appropriate in the school setting. This can be a serious obstacle, especially if we are trying to achieve a break from present routines and attitudes. In order to cope with this it may be necessary to do a good deal of preparation before the first occasion, so that the situation faced by the young people as they arrive is so different from usual that they are momentarily not sure what to make of it. We are really producing a momentary disorientation, a situation to which the normal expectations and behaviour may not apply. Then we need to move quickly and positively to establish a set of expectations appropriate to the new programme that we are introducing.

It can be helpful sometimes to move temporarily to a new setting, and the community rooms attached to some schools offer this kind of opportunity. It can also be helpful to change in some way the composition of the group, for example by bringing in a number of allies. This kind of temporary help may be offered by any colleagues available, students on teaching practice, or more experienced (though not necessarily older) young people.

Discussion and Participation in Groups

Continuous individual participation in groups as large as twenty-five to thirty is difficult to achieve, and the ability to work in small groups within the larger group is fundamental to this kind of work. This applies as much to the formation of small support groups as it does to active participation in discussion.

Socratic Group Discussion

There are some simple techniques, designed to engage as many as thirty or more young people in simultaneous discussion, which I have called Socratic group discussion. We are all very conscious of the difficulty of engaging large groups in open discussion. Fear seems to be an important impediment – fear of making a fool of ourselves; uncertainty about how our contribution would be received; and fear of ridicule. There is also a formality about large groups, which leads not so much to a dialogue as to a series of statements by one person after another. And yet the same people will chatter happily if the group is small and intimate, and in this case the discussion has much more of the cut and thrust of a conversation. So why not use small groups as the basis for the discussion?

How small is small? Groups of two can be too small to sustain a discussion; with three there may be rather more material available, but already one can be left out. With four there is an increasing chance of a member of the group being left out, and groups of five often seem to need a chairman. (I usually suggest threes, and not more than fours.) We need also to be conscious of how people are placed in relation to one another. One person may find himself in a strong position, or another be left out because the group are facing one another unevenly. If we direct attention to this, young people very soon learn about sensible placing.

By putting a series of questions to the small groups, we can engage them in step-by-step discussion. Put the question, allow a few minutes for the small groups to develop the discussion, and then call for an open exchange. The movement from a tongue-tied large group to the lively open exchanges when the groups report their discussions can be quite dramatic. There seem to be two major elements in the social processes that produce this change, this willingness to take part in open exchanges. The first is the element of rehearsal, testing personal statements in the small groups by the responses of the two or three other people. The second is the support that arises from having a statement accepted by two colleagues. Together these two factors greatly increase our confidence to offer a contribution for a wider hearing. Having identified these two elements, it is possible to reinforce their effect. For example, we can suggest to the small groups that they help one another to clarify statements, and encourage them in their mutual support, and in helping one another to express what they have in mind.

Much of the success depends upon the ordering of the material. What area or information do we wish to see covered? What are the steps in the argument? What kind of sequence is required? It is like making normal teaching notes, but turning statements into questions. The steps need to be small – the small groups must be able to make the jump from the platform that they have just established in the last discussion to the question offered for the new discussion. And the prompt needs to be clear. If the small groups are not into the new discussion within thirty seconds, then the brief may have been insufficiently clear or too complex. And if they have not done something with the question in, say, two or three minutes, then they have probably been set too big a jump.

The small group discussions are a preparation for open exchanges: we are using the discussion in small groups to explore the issues rather than to come to conclusions. We are teaching – not just conducting a discussion. It may be a disadvantage for the small groups to settle on conclusions, since they may be working on insufficient evidence. The function of the discussion in small groups is to explore – to 'rough up' the topic. It is only part of the process – the open exchanges carry the topic along further, and the person conducting the discussion will have ample opportunity to contribute to the discussion, and to feed in new evidence as well as to give rein to the views of the contributing groups.

The discussion is Socratic in a sense that a question is posed, the small groups engage in exploratory discussion, there is an open exchange which can be summarised, and this summary forms the basis for the next question. This means that the person conducting Socratic discussion must be able to foresee the likely course of the discussion in order to prepare in advance. With a little experience it is possible to anticipate much of the outcome of the discussion, but we cannot expect the ball always to be returned to our chest – we may have to reach out for it. It is a method of teaching, and we may be accused of manipulation. It is important that we should not only take other people's views into account, but also demonstrate that we are being influenced by them and that we, too, are learning from the discussion.

There is always a danger that little groups of friends will get together to have a cosy chat about their pop stars, or what happened yesterday evening. This will pass, and can often be overcome by the tempo at which the discussion is conducted. The questions should represent quite tiny jumps, and be committed to small group discussion for only a few minutes, brought into the open exchanges, and the next question be passed out briskly into small group discussion again. The tutor will develop a number of skills in conducting Socratic discussion. For example, the tone should be bright, occasionally humorous, but above all generous and supportive. And the tutor should observe the greatest economy in his own contributions: a few words too many from the tutor and down comes the tempo.

The tutor should be an active participant the whole time. When the question has been set and the groups have begun discussion, the tutor should join a group fairly unobtrusively. Avoid being just a silent observer – that can be somewhat threatening – but avoid also doing the work for the group. A prompt or a word of encouragement may be all that is necessary. The small groups may tend to defer to the tutor's presence at first, but a slight hand gesture will suggest that they carry on notwithstanding the tutor's presence. By joining the groups it is possible,

to check that the briefing is clear, understood and workable;
to help the groups along the line of discussion;
for the tutor to make himself accessible and shorten distance;
to identify contributions that would be valuable to the subsequent open exchanges.

The last of these is particularly important for a variety of reasons, especially in enabling the tutor to draw out individual young people who find it more difficult to speak in the open. In this the tutor's own placing is important. For example, in order to encourage a timid young person to make a contribution it may be necessary to stand close to him or her, to receive what is being said and relay it to the rest of the group. But next time the tutor will be able to stand further away, and before long the same young person may well be speaking across the whole group.

There will be a tendency for young people to address their comments to the tutor and only gradually will a real exchange develop across the whole group. This development can be helped along by a few simple techniques.

Deflecting. We do not respond directly to contribution addressed to us, but by gesture, by looking to others, or by a word or two, we pass the contribution for comment by other members of the group.

Drawing on. Again by gesture or a few words we encourage someone to enlarge upon a statement that they have just made.

Bouncing back. By a brief response, or by echoing part of a statement, we encourage the contributor to develop his argument.

Storing. An important ability depending upon the quality of our own preparation – if a statement is made that may have greater relevance to a later part of the discussion, we may only acknowledge the statement at this stage, and pigeon-hole it in readiness for the later discussion. When this is reached we may be able to revive the statement, so that another member of the group rather than the tutor initiates the new line of discussion. If you cannot trust your memory, jot down a word or two as an *aide-mémoire*. You may find it necessary to remind the contributor what it was that he said!

Changing direction. In changing direction smoothly we are again helped by our preparation. If we are clear about our direction, someone will usually offer the prompt that can be used for a change of direction, and the ability to store will be of special importance here.

Agendas. Numerous examples of agendas that can form the basis of Socratic discussion will be found in the programmes. Sometimes we are faced by groups who are so insecure, or unaccustomed to permissible talking in school, that they have difficulty in formulating the first few statements. Something very simple is required, and we sometimes need to have recourse to simple memory recall. For example, in leading into a discussion about relationships we may ask, 'Who were the first two people you met this morning? Help one another to remember.' Then, after some open exchanges, 'What did you say to one another? Tell the other members of your group.' And then again, after an open exchange, 'And how did you treat one another?' It is largely a matter of moving from memory recall at a concrete level to more abstract discussion.

The Use of Small Groups

Skills in Socratic group discussion, in both the tutor and the young people, serve as a key to so much else in these pastoral programmes. Once established, the skills of working in small groups can be used for a whole variety of purposes.

Brain Storming This is a way of producing as many ideas as possible in a short time. For example, brain storming can be used to produce ideas quickly for what could go into a year assembly, or items for agendas and enquiries.

Personal Support Groups Although it is true that there can be extremely supportive and personal exchanges in a total group of twenty-five to thirty, the number of people who can be at the centre of attention at any one time is clearly limited. If we can work through small support groups, this can increase the speed and intensity of the work very considerably.

It is possible to distinguish between exploratory and reflective work, and between corporate activity and small group activity. Much of the new experience will need to be initiated by the tutor in the corporate setting. Small groups may then be used:

to continue, at a personal level, the exploration that has been initiated through the corporate activity;
to reflect on the implications of the corporate experience;
to offer one another support in the declaration of personal objectives, in the planning of personal strategies, and in moving towards those objectives.

Firm contracts need to be made within the small groups to ensure that this level of mutual support is initiated and maintained. In most cases the size of these support groups has been from four to six young people.

Many tutors have found it possible to nurture some indigenous leadership from within the small support groups. They have not always used the term leadership, since leadership is often seen as synonymous with bossing. Many other expressions have been used to describe the leaders, such as representatives, chairman, and even facilitators. It can be established that the representatives of the small groups will serve in this function for, say, a term or half a term, or even as little as a few weeks, and that the role will be passed around the group.

These representatives serve as informal chairmen of the groups, and in particular should lead the support for individual members. Their sophistication and effectiveness can be rapidly enhanced by calling them together as a small working party. They will consider the way the programme is going, and any help that should be given to individual young people. For some purposes, the concern of the small groups will not be enough. For example, in the case of a number of fixed roles, such as clown or scapegoat, the support of the whole class may be needed before the person concerned can be released from the role and be encouraged to develop new styles of behaviour.

Academic Support Groups Some tutors use the personal support groups to support academic progress also, but it will often be found profitable to create a different kind of group for this purpose. The function is similar – individual young people are encouraged to declare their own academic objectives, and it is the job of the academic support groups to help their members to move towards those objectives.

This may involve helping one another to understand principles that are found difficult, to practice and to drill. It is important that the groups learn how to help one another without pre-empting individual effort. This will need to be the subject of specific discussion and practice, and will need regular reinforcement. Young people can offer one another tremendous support in this way, and the experience can be of as much value to the leader as to the led. The style of leadership within these groups is important. The function of the leaders is again to facilitate the work of the groups, rather than attempting to undertake the work themselves.

Communication Skills

The rapidity with which communication skills can grow is one of the most rewarding aspects of this work. It all begins as part of the meeting and greeting, and continues as specific conversation and listening exercises. It is important to focus strongly on the skills of listening. It is not generally appreciated that listening is active rather than passive, and that the listener frequently leads the conversation. He indicates his interest, by his feed-back he encourages the speaker to continue, and through his questions he may open new avenues for the conversation. The concept of outside experience is especially important in the case of social skills, and outside experience is suggested as an essential part of many of the exercises in communication skills. This enters even day one of the first year programme, where conversations within the group lead to preparation for reporting the experience to parents.

Agendas and Frameworks

It is important that the concept of agendas and frameworks is firmly established at an early stage. It is an essential step in helping young people to enlarge their conversational skills, and it is an important principle entering a number of other activities within the programmes. For example, a facility in preparing agendas and frameworks for conversation leads immediately to the preparation for receiving visitors. It is a basic skill also in preparing enquiries and action research. Ease in preparing outlines and frameworks is a considerable prize, for it is a skill that runs right through the young person's academic work. For example, it is very much easier to manipulate and re-order outlines and frameworks than completed prose. Note-taking represents the reverse side of this skill, and this is introduced into the second year programme.

Public Statements

The ability to speak to and in front of a group of thirty people is an important skill, demanding more self-confidence than many young people can muster. It is important in school work, since quite a lot of learning and practice is done through open exchanges in front of the whole class.

It is not difficult to help most young people in their attempts to make open statements to the whole tutorial group. It is closely allied to conversation skills and preparing agendas and frameworks. The skill needs to be approached step by step, as it is through these programmes. This is also part of the preparation of young people to play an active part in community life.

Role-play

Role-play in a variety of forms contributes very considerably to the experience of the young people following these programmes. It is vital that the tutor should be at ease in leading into role-play, and that the young people should turn naturally to role-play whenever this would be helpful. Its key position is illustrated by the way in which role-play enters even the first few stages of the first year programme. As early as stage two the young people prepare a conversation with their own tutor as a rehearsal for receiving an outside visitor. In stage three, role-play is used to practice approaches to several people who will be encountered in the orienteering exercise used to familiarise the young people with the layout of the school. And in stage four, the young people consider and practice ways of engaging the interest of their parents in what they have been doing in school.

Role-play should be conducted as spontaneously as possible, and be built up as it goes along. Be careful not to formalize it by too much prior explanation. For example, speaking to the whole group:

'So what will you say to your parents about what we have been doing, and how will you
approach them?'
There will be some tentative suggestions.
'Jackie, would you like to show us how you think it might go with you? Come and join me
here. Now whom will you be talking to first?'
Jackie responds.
'Your mother? Whom would you like to play your mother?'
A choice is made.
'Right, Janet, come and join us here.'
To Jackie: 'When will this be? What will your mother be doing?'
Jackie responds.
'Could you do that, Janet? Now, Jackie, show us how you will approach your mother.'
A few moments' role-play ensues and we might intercede.
'Is that how your mother would respond? Is Janet doing it correctly?'
And then we may ask the rest of the group:
'Now what about Jackie's approach?'
And the role-play quickly becomes an activated discussion.
'What do you think of those suggestions, Jackie? Would you like to try again?'
After a little development of the role-play we may wish to enlarge the scene.
'But what about your father and any other members of the family? Whom would you choose
to play your father?'
And so the role-play is developed.
In time we will want to extend the experience to other members of the group, and we may ask,
'Who else will show us how they will approach this?'

Several other examples may be played in front of the whole group. It is important that as
many people as possible should practise their approaches, and some young people could not at
the early stages attempt role-play in front of the whole group. So we shall soon need to arrange
for small groups to rehearse one another through role-play. In this way, it is possible in only a
few minutes for all the members of the group to practise their own strategies.

The use of role-play to work out strategies and practise personal approaches can quite
rapidly build up confidence and raise the level of what many young people can attempt. For
example, two young people are inviting a much feared senior member of staff to visit the group.
'Now, are you ready to take charge of Mr. X? He will be relying on you to bring him along.
You are the important people in this scene. Like to try again?'
And one can see young people grow visibly as the role-play proceeds, with the result that they
will be able successfully to tackle challenges that a few minutes before would have been beyond
them. It is important that young people should succeed, and the quality of the preparation is
vital to their success.

Role-play can be used also to explore personal styles of behaviour. Many young people are
unaware of how their behaviour strikes other people, and role-play is a way of gaining an
objective view of personal behaviour. For example, a young person has difficulty in hitting it off
with his (or her) peers. He has reached the stage when he can admit to his difficulties and would
like to try new approaches. The tutor seizes upon a moment to say, 'Show us what you mean',
and immediately sets up a brief role-play. It is like an acted discussion. Sometimes it will be
possible to stop a normal flow of events with, 'Did you see what happened then – let us do it
again', and a new objectivity can be brought into a view of recurring and perhaps unhelpful
behaviour. The discussion and role-play can immediately be extended to trying new styles of
behaviour, and contracts can be made to support the individuals concerned in their attempt to
change direction. It is unlikely to be possible to change a life style in a single stride, so it may be
necessary to envisage a series of steps. Attention to support and contracts, and the skills
involved in offering support through small groups, will assume great importance at this stage.

Role-play can also be used to explore the behaviour of a group as a whole. For example, any individual role will have its counterpart in the expectations of the people who surround the person playing that role, and it may be necessary to explore both the individual's behaviour and the group's responses. This can be true in, say, a case of scapegoating, or of someone with whom his (her) peers lose patience. Any occasion on which we can say, 'Show us what happened', can take us into spontaneous role-play. When role-play is used to explore group behaviour in this way it is often called socio-drama.

We can also explore the personal life space of one individual through role-play. What kind of relationships has he (she) to cope with daily, and how does he respond to the people in those situations? To what extent does he produce those relationships by his own behaviour? Through role-play, the individual may take us from one personal situation to another, bringing an unusual objectivity into his view of his own relationships and behaviour. When role-play is used in this way it is sometimes called psycho-drama.

Receiving Visitors

Introducing visitors into the group serves as a major vehicle for many vital experiences for young people. The term visitor in this context implies someone who is invited into the group, not to give a talk, but mainly to respond to the initiative of the young people. It is a natural extension of conversation skills, giving rein to the preparation of agendas and frameworks for extended conversations, and gives practice in meeting, greeting and coping with strangers of significance.

There is a great variety of experience inherent in the exercise. The visitor must be invited to come along, be met and entertained, be received by the group with genuine interest and consideration, be held in a sustained dialogue, and the occasion needs to be concluded gracefully.

The preparation for receiving a visitor needs to be good. Each person who is to play a part should be helped to plan his (her) approach through role-play. For example, the young person who is to receive the visitor and bring him to the group will role-play making contact and welcoming, and making the journey to the group. The long walk from, say, the entrance to the school to the room where the meeting is to take place is sometimes overlooked, and there needs to be some discussion and role-play of the kind of extended conversation that will be required. The tutor, serving as the role-play visitor, will prolong this walk by circling around the room several times, asking the young person who is to receive the visitor:

'Now, how will you keep the conversation going?'
And after a pause:

'As the visitor I am rather nervous too. I am not quite sure what is going to happen. Are you going to ask me awkward questions? How will you set me at ease and prepare me for meeting your group?'
Suggestions will be made by a number of the other members of the group.

'Let us try again.'

How will the group make the visitor welcome? There is sometimes a sheepishness to overcome, and the group often need to practise standing to receive the visitor, offering their hands and introducing themselves. Their competence in this respect usually grows rapidly.

As for the actual conversation with the visitor, the early occasions for this are usually concerned with meeting the visitor as a person, and the approach to this needs some careful thought. How can one express personal interest in the visitor without being too demanding and intrusive? It has been our general experience that visitors enjoy the interest expressed by young people in them as persons, and young people get a considerable satisfaction out of the exchange. Obviously, leading questions have to be prepared, and various members of the group will undertake responsibility for leading into different areas of conversation. A brief brain storming session usually produces all the prompts that are required.

The purpose of the prompts should be to open the door to the visitor to share a whole range of personal concerns with the group, but for him to feel free to chose just how much he divulges about himself. He will however require an invitation from the young people to share these personal interests with them, before it will be seen as appropriate to do so. The preparation for the visitor is therefore a natural follow-on from the preparation for personal conversations between the young people themselves.

Receiving visitors is a powerful experience. A great number of diffident young people have found strength as a result of the part that they have played in this exercise, and many disaffected young people have found it possible to identify with the group for the first time as a result of the responsibility that they have assumed, for example, for receiving the visitor or leading a certain area of conversation. It also gives great opportunity for the group to encourage young people towards experience that will be appropriate for their stage of development. If we ask, 'Who will receive the visitor?' we are likely to draw the nomination of the bolder and socially more able young people. If we change the question to, 'Who ought to be encouraged to receive the visitor?', we are immediately into a very different kind of exercise.

The amount and spread of experience can obviously be increased if we can find enough visitors for small groups each to receive their own, and it is usually not difficult to find a number of willing adults. For example, in school, the secretaries, the caretaking staff, the nurse, the catering staff, the welfare officer may all be pleased to take part, and this exercise also gives us an opportunity to bring in many other people who would be interested in making a small contribution to the school.

Once established, the visitor technique can be used for many purposes. For example, instead of bringing in a specialist speaker to deal with, for example, health education, the programme being followed by the young people can lead naturally to their inviting a specialist visitor to discuss the topic with them. In preparing to receive the visitor the young people will have already initiated a good deal of discussion about the topic. In this way the tutor will be party to the preparation, will share the conversation between the young people and the visitor, will lead the subsequent review amongst the young people of the experience, and will be available to continue the conversation with any individual young people or with the group as a whole. Many topics are approached in this way in these pastoral programmes, including health and hygiene, sex education, community interests from community service to vandalism, the welfare of the school, personal leisure time interests, careers education, subject choices and preparation for examinations.

It is important, when specialist visitors are invited, that the group should not neglect the personal side of the conversation. Having engaged with a visitor at a personal level, his (her) more specialist message has a new meaning, and the young people feel free to approach their side of the dialogue with a greater sense of personal interest and freedom. The initiative in the dialogue should still be with the young people, but the specialist will have considerable freedom to enlarge on themes that he (she) considers important. It is sometimes more difficult for the visitor than for the young people to accept the kind of restraints that a true dialogue implies, especially when the visitor has been accustomed to giving talks. The preparation of the visitor is vital, therefore, and the tutor may still need to hold the reins on some occasions, when the young people would have difficulty in coping with a loquacious visitor.

Visitors are used extensively in these pastoral programmes, and since there will be a number of tutorial groups in any one year, the number of visitors required will be very considerable. Some thought will need to be given to the accumulation and preparation of a bank of visitors. It is envisaged that the year head or other pastoral heads will be concerned with this, and other people in the school, such as any career specialists, can also make a contribution.

Action Research

This whole pastoral programme is enquiry based, helping young people to explore their own situations, the social forces that influence their behaviour and state of mind, and the alternatives open to them, including the paths towards any objectives that they may establish. This is not to say that they will do this uninfluenced or unaided, but the tutor's role is to feed their own self-discovery and not to pre-empt it. We are much more influenced by what we discover for ourselves than by what we are told, and this is particularly true of matters that influence our personal attitudes and behaviour. And pastoral work is very much about attitudes and approaches to life. So to some degree the whole programme is conducted through action research.

By action research I mean personal enquiry into the situations in which we find ourselves, or into any other factors that influence us or upon which we can have an influence. The approach can be aimed at several objectives at the same time. For example, as we consider what young people face when growing up, we can use action research to increase communication with parents, using the topic as a vehicle. We can at the same time help young people towards a realisation of the problems of parents in the adjustment that they, too, must make as their teenage sons and daughters grow up. The themes will increase in sophistication as the young people grow in their understanding, and the action research introduced in the latter part of the second year serves a number of themes at once:

(a) to open a dialogue with parents about the behaviour expected of young people;
(b) to consider the exercise of responsibility and authority in the community;
(c) to engage the interest and participation of parents in a parents' evening, to be staged and led largely by the young people;
(d) to consider the responsibility of young people in family life.

Action research includes an emphasis on *action* in a variety of ways:

(a) the participants are actively involved in the study of situations that affect them personally;
(b) an enquiry about a situation may already begin to influence that situation (an enquiry about communication between young people and their parents may already feed that communication);
(c) the discoveries that they make may move the participants sufficiently for them to want to do something about what they have uncovered;
(d) in taking action, the same spirit of enquiry will be continued, and in this way it will be possible to monitor the impact of the action being taken.

The scope for this kind of work is very considerable. For example, do we want young people to care for their school? Then should we engage them in some kind of enquiry about the welfare of the school? Do we want them to engage in some kind of community service? Then can we help them to uncover personal need, to which they can respond in a compassionate and intelligent way? Do we want to help them to be able to organise their homework time rather better? Then should we encourage them to undertake a study of how they approach their homework at present? Are we hoping that they might modify their group behaviour? Then can we help them to make a close study of how they are behaving at present?

Some care is required in guiding young people into action research. It is useful to think in terms of a number of steps:

1 Some way must be found of raising sufficient interest for young people to be moved to engage in the enquiry in the first place – an initial head of steam, as it were. Many opportunities will arise naturally out of these pastoral programmes, or a visitor may engage their interest in some kind of enquiry.

2 The young people will need to formulate their enquiry, and their experience of constructing

agendas and frameworks for themselves should make this fairly straightforward.

3 Try to keep the enquiry and the whole action simple, and well within the competence of the young people in terms both of their ability and of the time available.

4 Review the findings of the enquiry, and if their discoveries have real significance, the young people may well be stirred to action. Once again, sufficient head of steam needs to be generated at this point in order to maintain the momentum.

5 Not all enquiries will be intended to lead to action. Some may be designed in order to help young people to reconsider their own attitudes or behaviour.

6 The preparation for action needs to be thorough, especially if that action is likely to present a challenge to individual young people. Role-play the action, and engage the young people in clear contracts with one another to see the action through, possibly through small support groups.

7 The action taken should include an element of enquiry, so that when the young people return to review their progress, they are involved in new discoveries that may add further impetus to the undertaking.

Action research can lead to really potent experience – carrying through the enquiry, making contact with new people, being listened to when presenting their findings (which puts the young people in a strong position), and especially carrying through action that is seen to be of value to other people. For some it can be a boost to their self-esteem.

Much of the action research incorporated in the first and second year programme is short-term, with the intention of informing young people, helping them into important experience, and influencing their attitudes. A very early example of this is in the induction programme, where young people are encouraged to find their way around the school by orienteering. This is an example of a discovery programme, which attempts to place initiative and responsibility in the hands of the young people. Action research can also serve as a fulcrum for interlocking themes and programmes. The second year action research about other people in our community has a number of objectives.

(a) By involving the young people in immediate action, it feeds the idea that they should be participants within their own community.

(b) In looking at responsibility and authority in the community, it also asks questions about the responsibility of young people.

(c) By engaging the young people in an enquiry with their parents, it enhances the level of communication between them.

(d) In looking at people's interests and enthusiasms, it prepares for a discussion of leisure time interests.

(e) It provides an impetus to the young people learning how to conduct themselves in a formal meeting.

(f) It is part of the preparation for a parents' evening to be staged largely by the young people.

(g) It helps to engage the parents' interest, and their commitment to attend the evening, and raises several themes which are to be part of the discussion for that evening.

(h) It begins a consideration of the part that the family plays in community life, a topic that will be picked up during the parents' evening.

Relationships

We are what we are through our relationships with a whole range of people – our families, friends and associates, and even those whom we would prefer to avoid but are forced to meet regularly. And since relationships are at the core of life, it is not surprising that the relationships maintained by the young people are prominent in these pastoral programmes.

The ability to strike up easy and responsible relationships rests upon a number of attitudes and social skills. These social skills have to be learnt through practice. We cannot learn relationships by being told about them – the real learning comes from experience and practice. In order to help young people to develop creative and responsible relationships, we must help them into situations which give them the opportunity to practise those relationships. And because a relationship is always two-sided, any modification on the part of one individual must be matched by a change in the other people involved in the relationship. Which means that we may need to support young people in their efforts to negotiate a change of response from parents, friends and associates distant from our tutorial group.

The Family

The importance of the family and of the child-parent relationship has been well documented. But the secondary school years are a period when most young people begin to establish their independence. For some, it is a happy period of growth, adjustment and exploration, but with others it is a time of some stress and even turmoil. It is not always appreciated that many parents have as much difficulty in adjusting to a new kind of relationship as their teenage sons and daughters.

We have a great opportunity to contribute to creative family relationships through our pastoral work. Some of this can be reached through discussion and role-play within the group, and our effectiveness can be enhanced through action research. But it is equally important that the parents should feel themselves involved in the pastoral programme. Many opportunities for this are written into these programmes.

The use of terms such as 'family' and 'parent' in this context may seem to imply an assumption that all the young people will be living in two-parent families. This is clearly not the case. Some young people will be very uneasy in their family relationships – and that unease will not be restricted to those without one or either parent. We should not be tempted to avoid a discussion of family relationships because the topic may be emotionally charged, but rather make sure that it is dealt with sensitively and in a supportive climate.

Friendship

Satisfactory friendships are near the core of life, and there is a danger that any young person who is in difficulties with his friendships will be in difficulty in many other departments of life. It is for this reason that considerable attention is given to friendship throughout the five-year programme, and especially to the attitudes and social skills that enter friendship-making. It is not always appreciated that this equal give-and-take peer relationship is one of the toughest relationships to strike and maintain. It is often said that if the child-parent relationship is satisfactory, then everything else will follow. Our own researches have demonstrated that this is not always so, and that friendship with peers is a relationship that has to be learnt in its own right.

Most of this learning seems to take place early in life, in the rough and tumble of play with peers, and if it is not learnt at this stage it may be difficult to learn later. The lack of close friendships often leads to alternative coping strategies being built up and crystallised, and these may in themselves become an impediment to friendship making. This is sometimes expressed as an aloofness or superiority, and may lead to an attachment to the teacher or other adults. Any generally unacceptable behaviour that turns off other young people may become an habitual style.

We need to be on our guard about suggesting that having friends is a desirable thing. This depends very much on the individual, and only the people concerned can say whether they feel that life would be more satisfying if they were able to make friends more easily. Helping someone who wishes to develop the skills of friendship making usually requires a number of important steps. First the person needs to be able to look at his (her) own position objectively, and to have the confidence and daring to express the wish to change his position. Those who know him (her) well will need to be kind enough to help him see any way in which his own behaviour contributes to his difficulties, and a support group will need to help him identify alternative ways of behaving. He will then need to work out strategies by which he can practise new approaches and make new contacts. In doing this he may need considerable support.

Although the pastoral group may be a friendly group, it is much less likely to be a friendship group. Many of the members will have their real friends outside the group, and will look to the group for support rather than friendship. However, they may well befriend one of their members in need of help, whilst that person is finding his way outside the group.

Levels and Patterns of Friendships In conducting a discussion on the basis of the question, 'What do we mean by friendship?', we usually find that young people rapidly identify the elements of close friendship in terms such as the following:

> *Trust* – often in terms of exchanges about personal matters, but sometimes about money, or about not letting one another down.
> *Intimacy* – the sharing of deeper personal feelings, often described as secrets.
> *Acceptance* – being prepared to tolerate one another no matter what has happened.
> *Reciprocation* – for example, each using the other for sharing confidences. (This distinguishes a friend from a confidante – the confidante receives confidences but does not reciprocate in using the other partner as an intimate, as for example in the case of the teacher or counsellor.)

But young people will usually also suggest that not all their friendships are at this level, and they soon identify several levels of friendship:

> *Close friend* – someone you like and probably meet frequently, whom you trust and rely on, to whom you would confidently tell secrets – and expect him (her) to do the same to you.
> *Other friend* – someone you like and possibly meet frequently, whose company you seek, and who is more than an associate, but not a close friend.
> *Associate* – someone you may not go out of your way to meet, but if he (she) happens to be about you will join up with him (her) – sometimes called a casual friend.
> *Acquaintance* – someone you would acknowledge upon meeting, but would not normally choose as a companion for a social occasion.

We often portray this as in Figure 1.

It is important that the young people should not feel under pressure to suggest that they have a specific number of close friends in order to be normal, because individual people vary very considerably in their patterns of friendship. By concentrating on the first two levels of friendship – close friends and other good friends – Figure 2 portrays the variety of patterns that is likely to be found amongst any group of people. None of these patterns is right or wrong – they are just different. It is only the person concerned who is entitled to judge whether his existing pattern is comfortable and as he would like it to be.

Friendship, like so many other issues, is dealt with in this programme in a cyclical way, and the treatment becomes more sophisticated as the years progress. Some of the material outlined above is dealt with more fully in the working papers accompanying the programmes for Years Three and Four, suggesting that it is at these stages that a deeper consideration of friendship should occur. However, some young people may wish to consider friendship more deeply, and it is important that the tutor should be ready to respond to any urgent pre-occupations expressed by them.

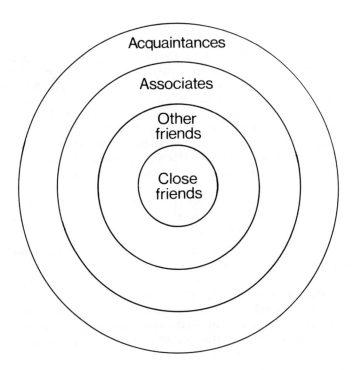

Figure 1 Levels of Friendship

Other Peers

Young people can be very insular and exclusive in their contacts, sometimes because they lack the skill and confidence to meet, greet and converse with other young people outside their immediate circle. Indeed, groups of young people can develop dramatic and unhelpful fantasies about outside groups. They can be helped to cope with strangers, and to make their way in less familiar circumstances. They also need to be able to cope with a variety of responses from peers, including hostility. A considerable amount of experience intended to help young people cope with peers who are strangers to them is structured into these pastoral programmes.

The ability to mix easily with the opposite sex may not keep pace with a growing sexual interest, which, as a result, may be expressed in an awkward manner. Some young people suffer excessive shyness in the presence of the opposite sex. In most tutorial groups we have special opportunities to enable boys and girls to meet and converse with one another at a personal level and in a graceful manner, without sexual overtones, and to learn kindness and consideration in their approaches. Occasions for this are structured into the pastoral programmes, with a progression to keep pace with their growing maturity.

Teachers, Other Adults and People in Authority

Relationships with parents and teachers inevitably involve feelings about authority. Many young people accept easily the authority that must be exercised by some of the adults with whom they are in contact, but at the other extreme, some young people react blindly to any expression of authority that touches them. They would blame the person in authority, but it is more likely that they are having difficulty in coping with the feelings about authority that are within them.

We need to give all young people an opportunity to consider their own feelings towards

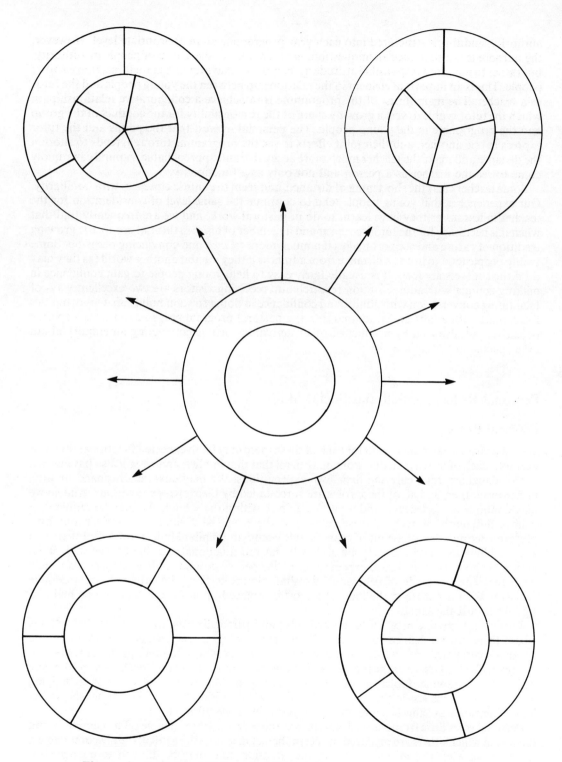

Figure 2 Individual Patterns of Friendship
Inner Circle – Close Friends   Outer Circle – Other Friends

authority, and this is structured into each year programme at an appropriate level. However, the purpose is not to induce an unquestioning acceptance of the action of people in authority, but rather to nurture a responsible attitude in their own behaviour and in their reaction to other people. This is an important element in the relationship between the young people and the tutor as a teacher. The main thrust of the programme is to achieve a collaborative relationship, in which the tutor is able to vest a growing share of the responsibility for the conduct of the group and the programme in the young people. The personal interest that the pupils and the tutor express in one another, and their joint efforts to see the programme through, tends to shorten the distance and make the teacher much more accessible and approachable. A pupil can rapidly come to see the teacher as a person and not only as a functionary.

Some teachers fear the shortening of distance, and seem to confuse closeness with familiarity. Our experience is that young people tend to continue the same level of consideration for the teacher in lessons as they have learnt to do in pastoral work, and we are frequently told that when it is necessary for the tutor to reprimand a member of his own tutorial group, the growing tradition of caring and support makes it a much more relaxed and convincing occasion. Some young people tend to live at a distance from adults as if they inhabit another world (as they may do if the contacts are few). It is usually fairly easy to help young people to gain confidence in making contact with adults. Action research and receiving visitors are two excellent ways of facilitating conversation with adults, and confidence in doing so soon builds up. Opportunities for contact with adults are structured into the pastoral programmes, sometimes as a specific objective, but also as a by-product of other activities, such as conducting an enquiry about other people in the community.

Personal Roles, the Self and Social Skills

Personal Roles

We play various parts in life, and for each of these there may be an expected functional role. For example, each of us is a man or a woman, with all that that implies; and we will also have been a son or daughter, roles carrying their own expectations. We may now be a husband or wife, father or mother, and all of these roles are surrounded by their own expectations. And so we may continue on to teacher, and a particular role within the school. We may be required to behave differently in each of these roles, and there will be a similarity between our own performance and the behaviour of other people occupying similar kinds of roles. But there will also be differences, because each one of us will play our functional roles in our own way, albeit within the bounds of the broad expectations of the people around us. If we depart too widely from the expected mode of behaviour, we shall almost certainly be subject to considerable critisism. We may chafe at the kind of limitations placed upon us, but they will be real and significant just the same.

There is a hazy line between functional roles and personal roles. In some social situations where there are no defined functions – for example, when a few friends meet to enjoy one another's company – we will still settle into roles, but these will be more personal roles. For example, we may be seen as the life and soul of the party, or the quiet one, or the wise bird. Some will assume pronounced roles such as clown or scapegoat. We give a lot of attention to bullying in school, but much less to the scapegoat who is bullied. It is quite possible that he (she) offers himself in this way, and has already developed a life style of doing so.

Personal roles arise from the push and pull of the way individual people offer themselves and the way in which others are prepared to accept them. Once roles are settled, they become subject to the expectations of all the people in the situation, and may be difficult to change. For example, in our studies and group work we have met many people playing a clown role who would like to be free to behave differently. But they find themselves forever reminded of their expected behaviour by the people around them. Unfortunately, as teachers we often become trapped in the same syndrome, and can find ourselves reinforcing the role, even by our attempts at correction.

This means that in order to help an individual out of a fixed role, those around him must be prepared to draw back – to modify their expectations – and give him (her) room for manoeuvre. But the person concerned may have only a limited repertoire of behaviour – having practised his role regularly for quite a number of years, he may have limited his own experience. Thus the clown may find it difficult to sustain a serious line of behaviour. This means that it is not enough merely to stand back and give room for movement: a support group must also help the person concerned to practise new ways of behaviour.

Some attention to personal roles is included in the pastoral programmes for Years One and Two, some of it explicitly about role behaviour, but also incidently in issues like friendship, and behaviour that may help or hinder friendship-making. The discussion becomes more sophisticated in the programmes for later years, but the needs of some young people may be so urgent in this respect that the tutor may find it necessary to focus on role behaviour quite specifically at an early stage of the programme, especially if established roles are causing destructive behaviour within the pastoral group.

Social Skills

All this adds emphasis to the importance of social skills in relationships and in a general life style. Practice in social skills is inherent in so much of the programme, but at certain stages the young people are invited to be deliberate about the development of their own skills. This occurs, for example, through self-description and a social skills workshop in the later part of Year One, leading to statements of personal objectives and strategies to meet those objectives. Tutors are likely to be encouraged by the rapidity with which many young people will be able to develop their social skills through the programme.

Self-Feelings

The way we play our part in life is very closely bound up with the way we feel about ourselves. These self-feelings are sometimes called self concepts. It is helpful to distinguish between the levels of self-feelings in terms of degrees of self-esteem, and the kind of person that we feel we are. Some people feel themselves as of very little worth, whilst others are easy with themselves in this respect. Our feelings about the kind of person that we are is closely allied to our feelings of worth, but may be expressed in a variety of ways. For example, one will characteristically be the odd man out, but the next will be the focus of attention. This is closely interwoven with the kind of personal roles that we establish.

In most cases these self-feelings are not entertained consciously, but they are none the less a very powerful influence in life. For example, a low sense of social worth can be very stultifying. Have you ever tried to persuade someone who does not believe that he can succeed that success is within his grasp? So often he will deflect every positive suggestion, but any negative evidence is accepted immediately. Similarly, those who feel themselves to be failures may well manoeuvre everyone into confirming their failure. Our self-feelings are deep within us, were probably laid down fairly early in life, and can be extremely resistant to change. Attempts at persuasion can easily be deflected, and more powerful experience may be necessary to help modify self-feelings. Here we are at a high point in our pastoral work: unless we can touch their self-feelings, we may find it difficult to help some of the young people in greatest need.

All this adds emphasis to the importance of the personal discovery and experience upon which these pastoral programmes are based. It can be valuable if, through personal discovery, an individual sees more clearly the way he feels about himself and the influence that this is having on his own life style. This will be approached with increasing sophistication in the pastoral programmes for the upper school. In the meantime, if the group can encourage young people to undertake roles through which they can experience being valued by other people, this can make a real impact on their self-feelings. This kind of experience can be inherent, for example, in assuming some of the roles to be played when the group is receiving visitors. To be valued by a supportive group can, in itself, be an enriching experience.

Group Norms

The expectations that we have of one another extend far beyond personal roles to the more general ways in which we are expected to behave in specific groups. For example, it may be appropriate in one class to co-operate with the teacher and school, but in another, such behaviour would be ridiculed by other members of the class. We use the term 'group norms' to describe the framework of expectations that is built up.

Group norms can work in very subtle ways, and the sanctions by which they are regulated can be built into the very fabric of the way the group normally acts. Some group norms can be helpful, but others can be very destructive. Teachers are faced by this every hour of the day, and only too often are victims of group controls in the classroom rather than the architects of them. Group norms are built up through the push and pull of the wishes of the various members of the group, and are coloured by the attitudes and expectations that the members of the group bring into the situation from outside. Once established, they may become both powerful and difficult to modify.

We regulate our behaviour by what we perceive the expectations of others to be, and there may be considerable miscalculation in this. For example, when within a group a number of young people may concur with the suggestion that school is a bore, but when questioned individually may reveal quite different personal views. It is possible for a whole group to conform to an expectation (for example, that as little effort as possible should be put into school work), and yet privately the great majority of the group will confess that they think that this behaviour is wrong. This means that they are miscalculating the wishes of the others, but since this is not brought out into the open the unhelpful influence of the group norm prevails.

Group norms may very well enter the response to the introduction of these pastoral programmes. For example, you may have difficulty with greetings and hand-taking. This is much more likely to be as a result of the expected reactions from peers than of any personal inclinations. In some groups, even support and trust may be difficult to establish because these are not the done thing in that group. We need to be very conscious of all this from the very outset of our work, and there are a number of points of entry built into these programmes. Some of them are implicit in other activities: for example, in 'How are we doing as a group?' (Stage 6). But others aim at making the influence of group norms explicit.

School Work and Responsibility in School

The emphasis of these programmes is on the young people's initiative, collaboration and responsibility, rather than on passivity and conformity. Clearly we need good order, but there are many opportunities to share the responsibility for maintaining good order with the young people. This is part of the distinction between discipline and obedience. In the first year programme, this responsibility tends to be expressed in terms of the caring and conduct within the tutorial group, but the second year programme is more outward looking, suggesting functions for the tutorial group in the wider school context, in year functions as well as in group functions, and finally in a parents' evening.

In order to encourage young people to take school seriously their views must be listened to, and with an attention that carries the conviction that the staff are taking these views into consideration. The visitor technique serves well here. It is important, too, that the younger pupils should feel that they have a stake in the responsibility for the school, and that this is not all vested in the older pupils. There are opportunities for the second year groups to share corporate decisions, especially about second year events. This tends to be more immediate than a rather more general and static school council. Arranging things on a year basis can allow a year to be responsible for a single or special occasion, with a new set of representatives being recruited for each venture in turn.

It is suggested that the young people should share responsibility for the year assemblies in the second year. Many schools already involve young people in the conduct of assemblies, but these pastoral programmes do much to lay the foundations for this to happen easily and fluently — through conversation skills, agendas and frameworks, public statements, small group discussion, brain storming and role-play.

School Work and Study Skills

It is hoped that one of the chief contributions of these pastoral programmes will be to the young people's academic work in school. In general, the programmes should release their willingness to work hard at their studies, with the support of their peers in doing so. Encouraging young people to take responsibility for their group, and for their own personal development, should flow over into taking a greater share of the responsibility for their own learning. Of course, our teaching methods will need to respond to this growing willingness and ability to collaborate.

In helping young people with their study skills a delicate balance will need to be maintained between what is attempted in pastoral time and what is appropriate to normal lessons. There are a number of areas common to all subjects to which the pastoral programme can contribute, such as conversation and communication skills, the ability to engage in class discussion, agendas and frameworks, and later, revision and examination techniques. The pastoral time is strictly limited, and it would be a mistake to presume upon areas that could be better served in normal class time.

It is particularly in the areas of attitude and anxiety that the pastoral programme can make the greatest contribution. Young people are encouraged to make their own assessment of their progress in school, to set their own objectives, and to establish strategies for reaching those objectives, including at times some consultation with specific subject teachers. This is the point at which the teacher-pupil relationship, to which the pastoral programme should make a very considerable contribution, assumes a special importance.

It is in facing themselves and their anxieties about school work that the support structure of the pastoral group can play a vital part. This is the reason that small academic support groups are suggested, who will learn how to help one another without undermining the need for individual effort.

File of Working Papers

It is most important that the young people should keep a file of completed working papers and other notes made during the programme. There is frequent need to refer back to previous statements and decisions.

3 The Teacher and the School

The Teacher's Leadership

There has been an emphasis throughout these notes on the collaborative rather than the directive nature of this work. Unfortunately, there is a tendency in the education service to equate non-authoritarian leadership with quiet or back-seat leadership. The style of leadership required for this kind of work is positive, often vigorous, but always feeding the initiative of the young people and not pre-empting it. The tutor's role should be one of encouraging and challenging, of showing our personal support and encouraging group support. This is a very active kind of leadership.

It is quite inevitable that the tutor will play a fairly central role, since he is leading young people to new experiences, and experiences that some might tend to avoid because they are challenging. So at one moment he will find it necessary to encourage and cajole, but at the next he may need to withdraw whilst the young people take up the initiative. But even his withdrawal will be a positive step in knowingly creating space for initiative by the young people.

Working on behalf of the School

The development of new approaches to pastoral work inevitably has implications for the total school programme, and it is vital that any experimentation should be seen as being undertaken on behalf of the school as a whole. There is a danger that if experimental work is undertaken privately – almost secretly – it will be denigrated by people who have no stake in it. There are a number of strategies that can be employed in order to keep colleagues informed, and the opportunities for this are built into the programme itself. For example, the visitor technique offers an excellent way of introducing colleagues to the work. The direct contact with the young people gives the visitor a sense of what is happening, and when personal contact has been made between the visitor and the young people, they usually respond to his questions about the experience with considerable candour.

It will be wise for the tutors who are to experiment with the programme to put their plans before a staff meeting before they begin work. The discussion may amount to no more than an acknowledgment that something is afoot, but they may well obtain their colleagues' agreement that the progress of the scheme should be monitored and reported. The formal appointment of monitors may be appropriate at this stage. Their role should be to stay close enough to the work to be able to understand what the tutors involved are attempting, the kind of response that they evoke from the young people, and the impact of the work on at least a sample of the young people concerned. They could be consulted about the choice of visitors, and take the opportunity of hearing from the visitors after they have met the young people. The monitors should also see any draft reports, and be encouraged to add their own objective comments either to the report or at a meeting at which the report is presented.

Some formal communication between the tutors involved and other members of staff having regular contact with the young people concerned can also be of great value in a number of ways. Young people will tend to be kept in their existing role, and they may continue to respond as they usually do to members of staff who are not party to what is happening in the group. A request to a member of staff, to assess whether any change is taking place in certain young people, alerts this colleague to the possibility of change. It can serve almost as a reversal of the labelling process.

Staff Development

Many of the teachers who initiate this kind of work in school will have had the benefit of some introductory in-service training. The training style by which the work is conveyed usually rests on the methods themselves. Learning new skills will be through actual practice, following a structured programme of work with a co-operative and willing group of young people, who are aware that they are contributing to the development of the teacher's skills. The training group will itself function as a supportive group, and incorporate the approaches into their own work together. Concurrent meetings of the training group will keep pace, step-by-step, with the work undertaken with the young people. The experience of the trainees will be examined, the principles of the work studied, and new approaches tried by the training group in readiness for the next assignment of fieldwork with young people.

Not all members of staff who will be involved as form tutors will be willing or able to attend in-service courses away from the school. For this reason the spread of the work throughout the school is likely to rest on school-based training programmes. These have some advantages in that those who are mounting the training are immediately to hand to support their colleagues in applying the methods in their own tutorial group.

We have to be realistic about all this. First, the methods must prove themselves before the school would be justified in expanding the work. Second, since there are usually many tutorial groups within a single year, it is usually wise to advance year by year. This gives scope for a certain amount of self-selection of the tutors involved if this is desired, and that can be valuable at the commencement of a programme when establishing a new tradition.

The concept of staff development may well be widened in the context of this work. There is so much room for helpers, who can encourage small groups of young people within the tutorial group, that a whole range of people can be brought into the tutorial sessions. For example, many schools have used the work as a new way of involving senior students, who gladly accept the preparation, training and the tutorial support required to support the work in the younger classes in the school. In a number of cases joint workshops have taken place involving both staff and sixth formers. The work can also make a contribution to staff development beyond the immediate concern with pastoral work. The form of training, the style of school-based workshops, and the establishment of staff support groups all has relevance to other facets of school life.

Evaluation and Reporting

Evaluative reporting is an essential part of introducing this kind of work into the school. To some extent, the means of evaluation are structured into the programme. Many of the steps are diagnostic, not the tutor's diagnosis, but the student's own diagnosis supported by the tutor. The young person tells himself where he stands, for example in his social skills, he sets his objectives and needs to remind himself about his progress. This means that many of the young people will be articulate about their own development, and could well be our best informants. This can be sharpened by using the kind of scaled assessment suggested in the Appendix (pages 179–83). Here a number of social skills are expressed in terms of a series of *continua* giving an opportunity for an assessment to be made from time to time. It is desirable that the young people should be involved in their own evaluation as an important addition to their experience.

When reporting make sure that you consider your readership, and address your report to those people. If you want to ensure that the report is read, seek an appointment with the people concerned, so that the report can be discussed at a meeting. And if the experiment is taking place with the knowledge of the whole staff, then the report should be circulated and presented formally for discussion at a staff meeting. Some of the techniques you use in your work –

Socratic discussion, for example – would contribute to the liveliness of the discussion at a staff meeting.

The Scope for the Work

The focus of these programmes is on the main stream of pastoral work, especially on the role of the form tutor, but the scope for developmental group work, both in and out of school, is very much wider than that. Special programmes can be mounted to meet special needs. The approaches can very profitably be brought into, say, the short stay residential courses offered by many schools. The methods are being used also in work with young people at risk, with truants, and with those who find it difficult to settle in school. For this purpose a much more intensive programme must be offered, in which there is a concentration on personal development for the first two or three weeks, with the academic element being stepped up as the young people increase their readiness to give themselves to it.

This kind of work shades into programmes for delinquents, especially through Intermediate Treatment. The same basic methods are used, although once again the programme must be considerably more intensive than the pastoral programmes outlined here. There is great scope for co-operation between the school, the education welfare services and the social services in this kind of work. They are all trying to serve the same young people, and the school can often offer a most important focus for the work. This has proved the case even for many of the young people who, in the normal routines, have been in difficulties with school. There are also many programmes for unemployed young people in which these methods are being used.

Too often there seems to be a separation between school and the outside world. The school is a major social agency that can serve as a focus for so many purposes, and the existence of skills in developmental group work in school can greatly enhance the contribution that the school can make to the neighbourhood. Nowhere is this more so than in group work with families and parents. Any school that assiduously follows these pastoral programmes will rapidly discover the goodwill and interest that arises from the kind of parent contacts suggested, especially the parents' evenings. For example, on a number of occasions we have been reminded by the parents of the young people following one of these programmes that they, too, are bound up with their children's growth or difficulties, and that something similar could profitably be run for them. Does this mean that our pastoral work should be addressed both to the young people and their parents in their common concern with the adjustments involved in growing up?

THE FIRST YEAR PROGRAMME

INTRODUCTION

The transition from junior to senior school is a landmark in the child's experience at school, and it is vital that he or she should feel settled, accepted and cared for from the moment that he or she arrives in the school. It is for this reason that this programme includes an intensive induction period during the first week of the Autumn Term.

INDUCTION AND SEQUENCE

It is suggested that the whole of the first day should be devoted to the induction programme, and that there should be at least an additional session on each of the remaining days of the first week. Beyond that point, this outline programme is based on the assumption that a period of not less than thirty-five minutes each week will be set aside as a form period, and that the work can continue on at least two registration times of, say, fifteen minutes each. There is enough material in the programme to occupy more time than this if it is available.

TRAINING AND SUPPORT

In writing the programme, a familiarity with a number of techniques, strategies and concepts has been assumed, and some basic training in these elements is seen as a pre-requisite to launching a programme of this kind.

PLANNING SCHEDULES

A planning schedule precedes the block of programmes for the first day, for the first week, and for each half term. It will be seen from the planning schedules that a number of themes are intended to run right through the five year pastoral programmes. Each phase of work has its own points of emphasis, and this can readily be seen on the schedules. The emphasis given to the topics included in each stage is indicated on the planning schedule by one to three asterisks.

THE PROGRAMMES

Each stage represents the kind of programme that might be accomplished during a single week, and it is recognised that the school or pastoral team may wish to add certain administrative or other matters to the various programmes. There is a rounded flow of activity appropriate to the span of each half term.

The programme for each stage is laid out in the left-hand column, with objectives and suggestions for the tutor in the right-hand column. The programmes are supported by a set of pastoral Working Papers (to be found between pages 77 and 98), and references to these are by numbers in the text.

The use of the symbol● indicates that a copy of the Working Paper is needed for each pupil.

PLANNING SCHEDULE: YEAR ONE
Autumn term   *The whole day is devoted to the Induction Programme*

THEME	STAGE 1	STAGE 2	STAGE 3	STAGE 4
The pupil's place in the school	The form teacher as part of the group.*	Meeting the form teacher.**	Exploring the school.***	Receiving a visitor—some other person from within the school.**
Caring community	Getting to know one another. Support and trust.***	Support and trust. Getting to know more people.**	Trust, caring. Contracts.*	Meeting some new people in the form.*
Relationships, the self and social skills				
Communication skills	Meeting and coping with people.*	Developing conversations. Listening.**	Role-play. Meeting outside people.*	Conversation with visitor. Prepare to report to parents. Consolidate role-play.**
School work and study skills				Lesson programme —timetable.*
Academic guidance and careers education				
Health and hygiene				
Personal interests				

STAGE 1   *First Day*

PROGRAMME

Link hands – one hand – with someone you know.
Now give the other hand to someone else (if there is anyone else).
Is there anyone left out?
   Would someone offer a hand?

Now meet three new people – one after another.
   Take the hand of each one, and ask him or her:
      Who are you?
      Where do you live?

Now meet three more people – one by one.
   Again take the hand of each one, and add to your questions:
      What junior school did you go to?

Contracts (see page 5) – caring and support – discussion in small groups (see page 8) with some open exchanges.
   Form small groups of three or four.
   Discuss in your small groups:
      How can we make everyone feel that this is a good group to be in?
      How can we make this a caring group?

Join hands with the other people in your small group as a sign that we are here to help and support one another.

Trust Walk (see pages 6–7)

Break time:
   Do we know where to go and what to do?
   Can we find the toilets?
   How do we make sure that everyone is all right at break time?

OBJECTIVES AND COMMENTS

Establishing an interest in the other members of the group. Helping members to meet one another, and to see everyone is included. Acclimatizing the young people to hand taking.

Extending acquaintances by meeting new people in the group.
   First steps in conversations.
The teacher will take part and meet as many of the pupils as possible. Look out for those who find meeting others difficult.

Keep the movement going. Conduct the programme at a lively pace.

Focus on the purpose of the group as a caring group, and the significance of making contracts with one another.

Hand-taking as a symbol of trust and support.

Focus on trust and support.

Making sure that everyone is secure in the first venture into the wider school.

STAGE 2

First Day

PROGRAMME

Getting to know a few more people:
Take the hand of someone you have not met yet, and find out
– his/her name;
– where he/she lives;
– what junior school he/she went to;
– what gives him/her most pleasure.
Now meet two more people – one at a time – and do the same again.

Conversations – agendas (see page 12):
Form small groups of threes and fours for discussion and open exchanges. What are the interesting things we ought to find out about one another? Reports: Should we write down some of these suggestions?

Conversations and listening:
Take a partner.
Find things out about your partner using the suggestions already discussed.
Don't forget that listening means *encouraging* by showing that you are interested.

Getting to know the form teacher (as practice for coping with adults):
Get into fours to consider prompts (refer back to the suggestions made before). Get some kind of order in the topics. Hold a conversation with the form teacher.

Lunch time:
Does everyone know where to go and what to do?

OBJECTIVES AND COMMENTS

Extending acquaintance with the class.
Reaching out to people.
Encouraging boys and girls to meet one another.

Beginning to build a framework for conversations.
Help the class to work in small groups and to exchange the ideas thrown up in the small groups through open exchanges.

Learning to sustain conversations, especially at a personal level.

Focus on listening as an *active* process.

Dialogue with form teacher as preparation for a series of conversations with teachers and other adults.

STAGE 3   *First Day*

PROGRAMME

Greetings:
    Meet several new people.
    Hand-taking as a symbol – trust, caring, support, contracts.

Meet some older pupils who will help us as we explore the school.

Exploring the school:
(Use **Working Paper 1**, page 78, as an agenda.)
    Orienteering in groups of about five, generating self-help in making our way around the school. (Older pupils should be placed at strategic points.)
    Role-play (see pages 12–14) our approach to the people to whom we must report.

Return to base and report about the experience.

    Prepare statements in small groups for exchange between the whole class:
        Did we reach all the places to which we were directed? Were we well received by the people we had to meet? Did we conduct outselves in a responsible way? How did it feel, finding our way around the school?

OBJECTIVES AND COMMENTS

Extending the acquaintance of people in the classroom.
    Focus on trust, caring, support and contracts.
    Reiterate the importance of making contracts.

Making contact with older pupils, who have been briefed to support the orienteering exercise.

Coming to know the geography of the school through the pupils' initiative and discovery.

Ease of contact with people outside the group. (Introduce role-play for the purpose of rehearsal.)

Building a sense of self-help, and of self-discipline and personal responsibility.

Extending the skills of small group discussion and reporting to the whole class.

STAGE 4   *First Day*

PROGRAMME

Greetings:
> Find someone whom you have not already met.
> Take him or her by the hand.
> Settle down for a short conversation with that
> person. What kind of agenda will you use?

A visitor:
> In small groups, suggest the kinds of questions
> that you will ask in order to start a conversation
> – to get to know the visitor as a person; – to learn
> something about what he/she does in life. Settle
> the questions. Who will ask what? Who will
> receive the visitor? Role-play this. Who will
> conclude? Role-play this. Receive the visitor.
> Review how the group managed.

Prepare to report the first day in school to your
parents. Role-play your approach.

Check lesson timetable for tomorrow.

OBJECTIVES AND COMMENTS

Meeting a new person in the class, and practising
conversations.

Learning how to prepare to receive a visitor. This
needs careful preparation (including adequate
role-play). This is an exercise in engaging someone from outside the group in sustained
conversation.

Visitors could be drawn from anywhere in the
school – secretary, caretaker, teacher, technician,
librarian – or from outside the school too. Careful briefing of the visitor is also important.

The preparation for a report to parents could
consolidate the experience of role-play. After an
initial demonstration, small groups could provide
an opportunity for role-play for each of their
members.

PLANNING SCHEDULE: YEAR ONE
Autumn term

A stage (approximately 35 minutes) for each day

THEME	STAGE 5	STAGE 6	STAGE 7	STAGE 8
The pupil's place in the school	Getting to know about the school – prepare for visitor.**	Receiving a visitor —a pastoral head.***	Visit to the office —role-play.**	Dealing with emergencies in school —role-play.**
Caring community	Meeting some more people in the class.*	How are we progressing as a group? Renew contracts.*	How should we care for the people in our class?**	Work out caring routine.*
Relationships, the self and social skills				
Communication skills	Reporting conversation with parents. Listening.**		Communication with officials in the school.*	Prepare for report to parents.*
School work and study skills		Check lesson timetable and homework schedule.*		Are we clear about the lesson programme?*
Academic guidance and careers education				
Health and hygiene				
Personal interests				

STAGE 5

PROGRAMME

Greetings:
>   Meet one or two new people and hold a few minutes conversation with each.

Conversations in twos – how good are we becoming at conversation at a personal level?
Introduce partners in fours in the first person, putting ourselves in their shoes. How good are we at listening?

Report conversations with parents – role-play as appropriate.

Prepare for a visitor – perhaps a pastoral head?
>   What are the questions we want to ask about
>   – the visitor as a person?
>   – the school?
>   Who will invite the visitor?
>   Who will introduce him/her?
>   Who will conclude?
>   Role-play the scene.

OBJECTIVES AND COMMENTS

Deepening association in the classroom.

Focus on conversation and listening.
>   Emphasize the active, encouraging side of listening. Give practice in empathy.

Support communication about school with parents.

Preparing for a visitor (increase experience of role-play). This should be seen also as an opportunity for a senior member of staff to come to know and be known by the young people.

STAGE 6   *First Week*

PROGRAMME

Greetings:
  Look for anyone you have not yet met – have a
  few minutes conversation with him or her.

Revise preparation for visitor:
  (a) interest in him/her as a person;
  (b) about school;
  (c) check agendas; decide who is to initiate each
      topic;
  (d) revise role-play of introductions and
      conclusion.

Receive the visitor.

Review performance with visitor:
  (a) How well did we cope?
  (b) What did we learn?

Check lesson timetable and homework schedule.

How are we doing as a group?
  Brief discussion in small groups and open
  exchanges.

Final hand-taking and restatement of contracts.

OBJECTIVES AND COMMENTS

Extending ease and acquaintance in the class.

Coping with an authority figure as visitor.

Clearing queries about school.
  (Some prior discussion about important areas of
  consultation is necessary.)

Make sure that pupils are at ease with their lesson
  programme and homework schedule.

Help the group to share responsibility for their own
  progress as a group.

Reinforce contracts.

STAGE 7

PROGRAMME

Greetings:
Do you know everyone in the class? Greet anyone you do not know.

Have we established ourselves as a caring group? Small group discussion and open exchanges.
(a) Are there any special circumstances in which some of our group may need care and encouragement?
(b) How are we going to check that everyone is here?
(c) What should we do when people are ill?
(d) Are there any other difficulties that we should look out for?

How do we cope when we have to go alone to somewhere or somebody in the school?
Role-play a visit to the office, first as a demonstration and then in small groups.

OBJECTIVES AND COMMENTS

Extending the acquaintance in the class.

Arranging a caring *routine*, for which the pupils will share responsibility.

Coping with individual action in the school.

Introducing role-play in small groups, with members of the groups rehearsing one another.

STAGE 8

PROGRAMME

Greetings:
  Look for people we do not know. Have a few minutes conversation with a new person.

Where do we go when something has to be dealt with at once, such as
  – a cut or bruise or illness?
  – lost property?
  – a dental appointment?
  Small group discussion.
  Role-play some approaches.

Prepare for conversation at home reporting on our first week.
  Small group discussion to consider what to report. (Role-play approaches to parents.)

Are we clear about the lesson programme for next week?

Farewells at the end of our first week together, and good wishes for the week-end.

OBJECTIVES AND COMMENTS

Getting to know more people.

Coping with emergencies.

Developing ease in approaching adults and authority figures.

Extending the experience of role-play.

Nurturing communication with parents about school.

De-fusing anxieties about the lesson programme.

PLANNING SCHEDULE: YEAR ONE
Autumn term

A stage for each week, commencing second week

THEME	STAGE 9	STAGE 10	STAGE 11	STAGE 12	STAGE 13
The pupil's place in the school	What else do we need to know about school? Preparing for a visitor.*	Receiving a senior member of staff as visitor.***			
Caring community	Caring in action.*	Review caring routine.**	Renew support and contracts.**	Meeting someone new.*	Adieus and good wishes.*
Relationships, the self and social skills			Having friends.*	Friends in and out of the classroom.**	
Communication skills	A framework for a conversation with the visitor.**				
School work and study skills	Review lesson programme. Check homework schedules.*		Coping with homework —anxieties, approaches.*	How are we progressing at school? First self-assessment.**	How are we progressing in school? Second self-assessment.
Academic guidance and careers education					
Health and hygiene					
Personal interests					What will you do with your half-term holiday?*

STAGE 9   *Autumn Term*

PROGRAMME

Greetings.

Caring routine in action:
    (a) absences,
    (b) illness,
    (c) welcoming members back after illness,
    (d) difficulties inside or outside school.

Preparation for visit by a pastoral head or member
of management team.

    (a) Prepare agenda for personal conversation.
    (b) What is his/her role in the school?
    (c) What do we want to know about the school
       (e.g. programme – timetable, rules, what is
       expected of pupils)?

Who will introduce and who will conclude?

Review lesson programme. Check homework
programme.

OBJECTIVES AND COMMENTS

Initiate caring routine to involve pupils,
    e.g. with a small caring group who will remind us
    about what needs to be done.

Careful preparation for discussion with visitor both
    at personal and school level.

Ventilation of uncertainties and anxieties about
    school.

An opportunity for the visitor to come to know the
    young people – careful briefing is important.

Clear up any anxiety or confusion about lesson and
    homework programmes.

STAGE 10   *Autumn Term*

PROGRAMME

Greetings:
    Review the caring routine – does it work?
    How should we welcome any newcomer into the
    form?

Receive visitor:
    (a) revise preparation;
    (b) role-play reception and conclusion;
    (c) conversation with visitor.

Review the group's performance in receiving the
visitor:
    (a) what did we learn?
    (b) how well did we cope?

OBJECTIVES AND COMMENTS

Special attention will be needed in order to initiate a
    caring routine. The interest of the whole group
    should focus on the way it is to operate, e.g. who
    will follow up illnesses or hospital cases?

Concentration on receiving an authority figure as a
    visitor, and getting information about the school.

Work through discussion in small groups with
    statements to the whole class.

Encourage the small groups to look after their own
    members – including their contribution to the
    small group discussion, and to the open state-
    ments from the group.

STAGE 11
Autumn Term

PROGRAMME

Greetings and caring.

Renew trust – support – contracts – trust walk with someone different.

Having friends – small group discussion with open exchanges. What do we mean by having friends? What makes someone a friend? Do we have special friends? Who are those friends? (Discussion, followed by **Working Paper 4**.)

Homework – explore through discussion in small groups and open exchanges. How long did your homework take last night? Is this usual? Did you get stuck over anything? Have you been anxious about any of it? When do you do your homework? What is your routine?

OBJECTIVES AND COMMENTS

Renewal of contracts in readiness for discussion of friendship.

Serious discussion to see how school is affecting friendships. The completed working papers will help the tutor to gain an insight into how individual young people are placed in their friendships. A copy of **Working Paper 4** will be required for each pupil.

Try to de-fuse anxieties about homework. Begin discussion about organisation and method in tackling homework.

STAGE 12
Autumn Term

PROGRAMME

Greetings:
Have a conversation with someone new. How good are we at personal conversations now?

Caring.

Support – rocking in twos (see page 7).

Friends:
Is this a friendly form? Where are our friends – in the form or out of the form? Has everyone here got enough friends? Do we know people without friends? Would it be possible to be friendly with them?

How are we doing at lessons? (Use **Working Paper 8** – first self-assessment.)
Discussion in small support groups, followed by the completion of the self-assessment form.

OBJECTIVES AND COMMENTS

Consider progress in conversation skills.

Are the established routines proving effective?

See whether there are friendless people who might be supported by their classmates. The tutor's preparation will include a study of the completed working papers from Stage 11.

Look at anxieties surrounding school work, and any serious falling behind.

The teacher will need to collect and examine the completed assessments, which are as much to inform the school as to interest the pupil. The assessment continues in Stage 13. A copy of **Working Paper 8** will be required for each pupil.

STAGE 13

Autumn Term

(*Last stage before half-term break.*)

PROGRAMME

Greetings and caring.

How are we doing at school?
A discussion in small groups followed by the completion of the second self-assessment: **Working Paper 9**.

Review the summary of the two assessments and consider immediate action to be taken.

What will you do with your half-term holiday?
There should be
(a) some statements about plans;
(b) some information and discussion about personal interests;
(c) some kind of contribution by the form teacher.

Adieus and good wishes for the half-term break.

OBJECTIVES AND COMMENTS

To complete a review of school work.
First conduct a discussion using the working paper as an agenda.

The tutor should collect the completed papers for scrutiny. A copy of **Working Paper 9** will be required for each pupil.

The pupils' objectives should be carefully considered and will need to be reviewed after the half-term break.

To raise interest in a profitable use of holiday time.

PLANNING SCHEDULE: YEAR ONE

THEME	STAGE 14	STAGE 15	STAGE 16	STAGE 17	STAGE 18	STAGE 19	STAGE 20
The pupil's place in the school		A member of senior staff as visitor—his role in school.***				A senior member of staff as visitor.***	
Caring community	Greetings. Renew contracts. Caring in action.**	Meeting someone new. Build caring routine.*	Meeting someone new. Caring routine.*	Greetings. Check routine for caring.**	Is there anyone in the group whom we have not met?*	Making sure we know everybody in the group.*	Adieus and good wishes.*
Relationships, the self and social skills			What do we like about our friends?**	What gets in the way of people being friends?***			
Communication skills	Extended agendas and conversations. Preparation for visitor.**	Coping with visitor.*			Preparing for a visitor from the senior staff.*	Preparing for a report to parents.**	Reporting conversations with parents.**
School work and study skills	Timetable and homework schedules. Progress in lessons.*	Progress in lessons.*	Review home-work (a) schedule; (b) routines at home.**		How are we doing at school?***		
Personal interests					Looking forward to Christmas holidays—prepare for discussion in Stage 20.*		Interesting things to do at Christmas—discussion.**

STAGE 14   *Autumn Term*

(First stage after half-term break.)

PROGRAMME

Greetings:
  Meet most of the people in the class.

Caring:
  Is everyone here? Is there any illness or other
  reasons for absence?

Conversation in threes:
  (a) Agenda – what do we want to know from one
      another about the half-term holiday?
      (Reports to whole group.)
  (b) Conversation – and find out something new
      about our partners.

Prepare for visitor at the next session (member of
management/pastoral team):
  (a) Interest in the visitor as a person.
  (b) Some enquiry about his role in the school.

School programmes:
  (a) Check timetables.
  (b) Homework schedule.

Progress in lessons – working in small support
groups:
  (a) Review the objectives stated as a result of the
      self-assessments in Stages 12 and 13.
  (b) Help one another to plan individual action to
      approach these objectives.

OBJECTIVES AND COMMENTS

Make a special effort to renew contracts after the
half-term break.

Reinforce routine for caring.
  Decide about action and initiative required.
  Reconstitute the caring group if appropriate.

Extend the agendas for conversations.
  Reiterate the need to help one another in small
  group discussion.

Continuing practice in meeting people in authority
  in the school, and an opportunity for a senior
  member of staff to meet the young people.
  Further practice in extended agendas for
  conversation.

Make a quick check that everyone is clear about
  classwork and homework.

The tutor will have checked through the two self-
  assessments (which need to be returned to the
  young people for this exercise).

Engage the small groups in serious discussion about
  helping one another to move towards their
  objectives.

STAGE 15

PROGRAMME

Greetings:
  Meet someone new in a short conversation.

Caring:
  Report about action taken. Review attendances and wellbeing.

Receive a visitor:
  (a) Revise preparation.
  (b) Role-play reception and conclusion.

  Conversation with visitor.

Review group's performance in receiving visitor:
  (a) What did we learn?
  (b) How well did we cope
     – with receiving him/her?
     – with the conversation?
  (c) How are we progressing in receiving visitors?

Progress with lessons:
  Small support groups and open exchanges.
  (a) Review of objectives.
  (b) Action being attempted.
  (c) Statement of any serious difficulties.

OBJECTIVES AND COMMENTS

Extending acquaintance in the group.

Emphasise the responsibility of the group for caring for their members.

An opportunity to meet an additional member of the senior staff, and consider his/her view of the school. Brief the visitor carefully, so that he/she can respond helpfully to individual young people.

Deliberate review of progress in coping with visitors.

Reinforce self-help and mutual support on the part of the pupils.

The tutor needs to be alerted to obstacles that individual pupils are unable to overcome.

STAGE 16

Autumn Term

PROGRAMME

Greetings:
  Meet someone new.

Caring:
  Report and action.

Friendship:
  Small group discussion and open exchanges. Why are friends so important? What do we like about our friends?

Homework:
  (a) Check homework schedules.
  (b) Compare routines for tackling homework at home. (Small group discussion and corporate exchanges.)
  Where do we do it?
  When do we do it – does it hang over our heads?
  What else do we want to do with our evenings?
  How should we fit it all in?

OBJECTIVES AND COMMENTS

Extending contacts within the group.

Deepening a sense of responsibility in the group for its members.

Initiate some discussion about friendship making – the positive things about having friends.

Help members of the group to consider their approach to homework.

STAGE 17

Autumn Term

PROGRAMME

Greetings.

Caring:
  Report and consider any necessary action. Review arrangements for caring.

Friendship:
  What gets in the way of people making friends? Small group discussion and open exchanges.
  Is it:
  (a) the lack of opportunities to meet?
  (b) shyness or not being able to meet people?
  (c) the way some people behave?

  Can we help ourselves, for example, to meet and talk with other people easily?
  Are there any lonely people who could be befriended?

OBJECTIVES AND COMMENTS

Consolidate caring as a *regular* responsibility of the group.

Penetrate some of the difficulties that may be experienced in friendship making, and consider whether any help is required.

Encourage young people to reach out to others, for both their own and other people's benefit.

STAGE 18

PROGRAMME

Greetings:
Is there anyone in the group whom you have not yet met?

Caring.

Coping with difficulties in schoolwork:
Discussion in small groups with open exchanges as a preparation for receiving a senior member of staff as a visitor in Stage 19.

(a) Work through the agenda in **Working Paper 10**.

(b) Prepare matters to be raised with the visitor.

Personal interest:
What interesting things will you find to do in the Christmas holidays? Prepare for discussion and suggestions for Stage 20.

OBJECTIVES AND COMMENTS

Try to complete the contacts between members of the group.

A stocktaking of the term's work
(a) as a personal review for each member of the group;
(b) as the basis for exchanges with a senior member of staff as visitor.

Encourage members to think about the way they will be using their Christmas holidays.

STAGE 19

PROGRAMME

Greetings:
Make sure that we know everyone in the group.

Caring.

Receiving the visitor:
(a) Revise agenda for conversations.
(b) Role-play reception and conclusion.

Meet visitor.

Review the performance of the group in receiving the visitor.

Coping with difficulties in schoolwork:
What were the main suggestions that were made by the visitor to help us cope with difficulties? Discussion in small support groups and open exchanges.

Report to parents:
(a) What should we be reporting to our parents about our first term in this school? Small group discussion.
(b) Using the headings decided under (a), what will you report about your personal progress?
(c) Role-play the approach.

OBJECTIVES AND COMMENTS

Some emphasis on having met everybody.

Extend contacts with senior staff.

Consider areas of progress and malaise in school work, and discuss the pupils' approaches to their work.

Help the young people to focus on ways of helping themselves over their difficulties.
Have any matters been raised that will require wider staff consultation?

A deliberate effort to increase communication between the pupils and their parents about what they are doing at school.

Focus on self-assessment and reporting, and on the interests of parents in the pupil's progress.

STAGE 20

(*Final stage before Christmas break.*)

PROGRAMME

Greetings.

Caring:
How well have we cared for the members of our group?

Coping with difficulties in school work. Progress report – discussion in small support groups and open exchanges.

Report conversations with parents:
(a) How did the conversations go? Report in small groups and make some corporate statements.
(b) Role-play useful examples of approaches.
(c) How could our parents help us about school? Small group discussion and reports to whole group.

Interesting things to do in the Christmas holidays:
(a) exploration in small groups;
(b) individual statements to whole group.

Adieus and good wishes – move round, take hands and wish everyone well. Are there any arrangements for meeting some classmates during holidays?

OBJECTIVES AND COMMENTS

Consolidate self help. Report anything appropriate arising out of staff consultations.

Progress report may need to be stimulated by an agenda – the matters raised with the visitor might supply this.

Check the kind of communication possible with parents, and begin to cope with any difficulties in communication.

Explore the ways in which parents could be drawn closely into the pupils' school work and progress.

Encourage active use of holidays, and share interesting ideas for Christmas festivities.

Hear from small groups and individuals about interesting personal pursuits.

PLANNING SCHEDULE: YEAR ONE

THEME	STAGE 21	STAGE 22	STAGE 23	STAGE 24	STAGE 25	STAGE 26
The pupil's place in the school		Responsibilities in school.**				
Caring community	Review methods of caring. Reaffirm support and renew contracts.**			Extend support.*	Continuing support with personal roles.*	Support with personal roles.*
Relationships, the self and social skills		Relationships with other peers.***	Peers and relationships between boys & girls.***	Personal roles. Contracts for long-term support.***	Self—what is it like to be me growing up?**	
Communication skills	Reinforce agendas, Encourage public statements.**			Extended conversations.*	What should we be reporting to our parents?*	Report back.*
School work and study skills	Check lesson and homework programme.*		Check progress no snags or anxieties.**			
Academic guidance and careers education						
Health and hygiene					Growing up.**	Growing up —receiving a visitor.***
Personal interests						

STAGE 21

Spring Term

(First stage after Christmas break.)

PROGRAMME

Greetings:
Make sure that you take the hands of most people in the group. Renewal of support and contracts.

Caring:
Note absences and hear reports about general wellbeing. Re-establish the caring routine.

Check lesson and homework programmes.

What happened to you during the Christmas holidays? Enquire of one another in small groups.

Telling the whole group about something that happened during the Christmas holidays.

(a) How should you prepare for a statement to the whole group? Do you need steps, or a framework? Discuss this in your small groups – for example: when and where was it? Who was involved? What happened? What did it lead to, or how did you and other people feel about it?
(b) Now help one of your small group to tell the whole class about something that happened.
(c) Hear a short statement from each small group.
(d) Are we beginning to find it easier to speak to the whole class?
(e) Who finds it difficult? Could we help these people in any way?

OBJECTIVES AND COMMENTS

Give strong encouragement to bring the group together again, and to renew support and contracts.

Re-establish and reinforce the caring routine, and if there is a special group initiating the caring, revise its membership.

Use the exchanges about experiences during the Christmas break as a means of:

(a) renewing discussion in small groups;
(b) reinforcing the concept of agendas, and the skill in formulating them;
(c) encouraging confidence in making public statements.

STAGE 22
Spring Term

PROGRAMME

Greetings and caring.

Our responsibilities in school:
How are we coping as a form? (**Working Paper 2.**)

How do we get on with other boys and girls of our own age? Are we getting on with people who are not our friends? (**See Working Paper 5.**)

OBJECTIVES AND COMMENTS

Encouraging members of the group to behave responsibly during their time in school.

Extending the discussion about friendship to a consideration of how individuals cope with others of their own age.

Working Paper 5 should be used as an agenda for small group discussion. But if the tutor wants to follow up any of this information, each pupil could complete the working paper before, during or after the discussion.

Reference back to Stage 11, **Working Paper 4**, might be helpful.

STAGE 23
Spring Term

PROGRAMME

Greetings and caring.

Contacts between boys and girls:
Boys, do you know all the girls in this group, and visa versa? Let us move round again, and try to call all the boys or girls by name as we take their hands. Do you find a difference in greeting boys and girls? What makes it feel different? (Small group discussion and open exchanges.)

Conversations between boys and girls ('the way we see life') in mixed groups of threes and fours, using **Working Paper 6**.

Agendas:
What kinds of subjects would make a useful agenda for a friendly conversation between boys and girls? Small group discussion and open exchanges.

Progress in school (small group discussion and brief reports). I am having some difficulty with . . . . . I feel I could do better if only . . . . .

OBJECTIVES AND COMMENTS

Encouraging normal contacts between boys and girls.

Encourage all the boys to take the hands of all the girls and visa versa. Make room for any who find this too difficult – they should not lose face.

Consider people's feelings and confusions, and where these feelings may have come from.

Offer a firm agenda to stimulate conversations of a fairly personal nature between boys and girls.

Capitalise on the experience by encouraging the young people to foresee an appropriate framework for conversations.

A brief check to discern any snags or anxieties.

STAGE 24 *Spring Term*

PROGRAMME

Greetings and caring.

Getting to know another person – brief conversation between boys and girls in pairs.

Remind ourselves about support and contracts – rocking in twos. Encourage mixed pairs.

Our usual ways of behaving:
  (a) How does the teacher behave? Could anyone role-play this behaviour?
  (b) Divide into groups of four or five with people you know fairly well. Role-play one another's behaviour.
  (c) Is any of this behaviour unhelpful to the person concerned? For example, does he/she make other people fed up with him/her and spoil his/her own chances? – Small group discussion and some open reporting.
  (d) Could we help any of our members to change their behaviour in ways that would be more helpful to them?
  (e) Could we really support them in this, both in and out of the classroom?

OBJECTIVES AND COMMENTS

Follow up Stage 23 with practice.

Build up support in readiness for discussion about personal roles and behaviour.

Role-play the group tutor's behaviour to open up the situation.
Role-play in small groups to throw up any pronounced and unhelpful styles of behaviour.
If any person is to be helped, clear strategies will need to be worked out, both for a modification of the behaviour and for the support to be given to the individual.

STAGE 25

Spring Term

PROGRAMME

Greetings and caring.

Support in behavioural change:
  What kind of progress have we made? Are individuals getting the support they need?

Growing up:
  How are you finding it? See **Working Paper 12**, which can be used as an agenda for discussion in small groups (probably it is best to separate groups of girls and boys). The discussion and report should serve as a preparation for receiving a visitor in Stage 26.

What should we be reporting to our parents about our school activities? Prepare an agenda for a conversation through small groups and open exchange. Role-play the approach.

OBJECTIVES AND COMMENTS

Follow up any suggestions about changes in personal behaviours made at Stage 24.

A tentative self-description, focusing, in the latter part, on personal changes being experienced through puberty. An attempt to bring a discussion of often secret matters to an open, matter-of-fact level. Part of a double session – Stage 26 to involve receiving a knowledgeable visitor who can respond to the uncertainties and anxieties of the young people.

Helping the young person to play his/her part in conversations with parents about school.

STAGE 26

Spring Term

(Final stage before half-term break.)

PROGRAMME

Greetings and caring.

Report any progress in changing behaviour. Can we support one another during half-term holiday – and what about when we return to school?

Growing up:
Receiving a visitor.

(a) Revise the agenda and take responsibility for raising specific issues.
(b) Role-play reception and conclusion.

Receive the visitor.

(a) What did we learn?
(b) How well did we cope?

Conversation with parents:
(a) How did it go?
(b) Role-play how you approached it.
(c) Is there more that we should discuss with parents?

OBJECTIVES AND COMMENTS

Attempting to maintain the support to individuals into the half-term break and beyond.

Careful preparation is needed for the dialogue with the visitor who will respond to pupils about growing up and including their increasing sexual maturity.

Individual young people may need to be very well rehearsed.

It is important that the teacher is party to the conversation, so that it can be maintained as required later.

This is to help communication to grow, and will be followed up more directly in Stages 29 and 30.

PLANNING SCHEDULE: YEAR ONE

THEME	STAGE 27	STAGE 28	STAGE 29	STAGE 30	STAGE 31	STAGE 32
The pupil's place in the school	How are we doing as a group?**	Modification of group behaviour.**	How are we doing as a group? (Follow-up).*			
Caring community	Review methods of caring.*					Farewells and good wishes.*
Relationships, the self and social skills	Support behaviour change.*		Relationships with parents.***	Action research with parents.***	Follow-up conversations with parents.*	
Communication skills						Public statements (personal interests)*
School work and study skills					Third self-assessment. Strategies for next term.***	Consultation with subject teachers.*
Academic guidance and careers education						
Health and hygiene	Keeping healthy—preparation for a visitor.**	Keeping healthy—a visitor.***	Keeping healthy—application*	Keeping healthy—review.**		
Personal interests					Personal interests—including clubs, etc.*	Personal interests.**

STAGE 27   *Spring Term*

(First stage after half-term break.)

PROGRAMME

Greetings:
  Welcome back after the break.

Caring:
  Is everyone present and well?
  Review arrangements for caring.

How are we doing as a form? (Small group discussion and report.) Examples:
  (a) Punctuality.
  (b) Moving from room to room.
  (c) Attendance at assembly.
  (d) Being ready for classes and getting started with our work.
  (e) Tidiness and dress.
  (f) Is there anything that we are not good at as a form?
  (g) Do we face any special difficulties as a form?

  Note any matters that need discussion at Stage 28.

Reports to and conversations with parents. Report any follow-up of previous discussions in Stages 25 and 26. Small group discussions and open exchanges.

Keeping healthy:
  We are to have an opportunity of receiving a visitor who is knowledgeable about keeping healthy. What would we like to discuss with him/her? Construct an agenda, using small group discussions and open exchanges. Possible prompts for discussion are Food – Clothing – Exercise – Seeking medical attention – Rest and sleep – Cleanliness and hygiene, including teeth, feet, hair.

OBJECTIVES AND COMMENTS

A good recommencement is important.

Are changes required in the way that the caring routine is conducted, and in the people involved? If time is too short, this business may have to be completed in Stage 28.

A review of the way the form behaves as a whole and the kinds of group norms that have been built up. Preparation for modification of behaviour by discussion and decision in Stage 28, which would also include reinforcement of creative and helpful behaviour. The matters arising from the discussion in small groups should be noted as a basis for discussion in Stage 28.

Keep this interest warm in readiness for Stages 29 and 30.

The preparation of an agenda in readiness for a *dialogue* with a health education visitor in Stage 28.

STAGE 28

PROGRAMME

Greetings and caring.

How are we doing as a form? Small group discussion and corporate decisions about the main matters raised in Stage 27.

Keeping healthy – a visitor:
  (a) Revise agenda, to include personal interest in the visitor and a discussion about health.
  (b) Role-play receiving the visitor and concluding the session.

Receive the visitor.

  (a) Resumé – what did we learn?
  (b) How well did we cope?

OBJECTIVES AND COMMENTS

Complete any business outstanding from Stage 27.

It may not be possible to deal with all the matters raised – some can await Stages 29 and 30. In any case, some reinforcement will be required.

It is vital that the young people take an important share of the initiative – a conversation, not a talk, is required. The visitor should be fully briefed.

STAGE 29

PROGRAMME

Greetings and caring.

How are we doing as a form? Follow up discussions.

Keeping healthy:
Revision of what was learnt – how do we apply the points personally?

Our relationships with parents:
An action research programme, starting by formulation of enquiry through small working parties.

First determine the general areas of enquiry: e.g. What it is like to be a parent of a child who has recently moved from junior to senior school? What are parents' feelings about our time at school? What are parents' memories of their own childhood – fear, joys, embarrassments? How is the relationship between us and our parents changing? Could it be more rewarding for both?

Consider the possibility of a parents' evening next term. Having settled the headings, use the same small groups to finalise specific questions (see **Working Paper 7** for examples).

Role-play the approach, and encourage the members of the group to take the enquiry very seriously.

OBJECTIVES AND COMMENTS

Reinforcing considered behaviour.

Small groups consider the application to themselves of the main messages.

The purpose of the action research is:
– to enrich the communication between the child and his/her parents;
– to deepen a mutual understanding of both the child and the parent;
– to encourage the parent's interest in the child's school experience.

It is suggested that the formulation of the enquiry should be reached in two stages:
(a) settle the main headings through small working parties;
(b) formulate detailed questions by each working party taking one of the general headings, and suggesting prompts for conversation.

Examples of questions that may be appropriate will be found in **Working Paper 7**, which is intended only as a fall-back and to help with the teacher's preparation.

The conversation with parents will need careful role-play and preparation. Some members of the group may wish to combine together in interviewing.

Clear contracts to undertake the conversations need to be struck, possibly supported by final handtaking and good wishes.

STAGE 30   *Spring Term*

PROGRAMME

Greetings and caring.

Action research with parents:
How did it go? (Small groups preparing for open exchanges.) What kind of experience was it – for you? – for your parents?

Show us what happened. (Give examples in role-play.)

What were the most important things you found out? (Small group discussion preparing for open exchanges.)

What did you find out about:
(a) what it is like to be a parent of someone of your age?
(b) parents' memories of being your age?
(c) parents' feelings about their time at school?

What did it suggest to you about:
(a) the part that you should be playing in the relationship with your parents?
(b) the kind of steps we might be taking to build links between parents and school?
(c) how the communication at home can be developed?

Action – discussion in small groups:
What do we each need to do? Declare your own decision about action. How will you put your decision into effect?

Keeping healthy:
Progress report – how are we applying what we learnt? For example, what are we doing about food, exercise, rest and sleep, cleanliness and hygiene?

OBJECTIVES AND COMMENTS

Capitalise on the discoveries made through the action research with parents.

Crystallise the main points of learning, especially those that have moved and caught the imagination of the young people, and focus on the action required in response to these discoveries.

Engage young people in considering their part in creative family relationships.

Help the young people to plan their strategies, and prepare, e.g. through role-play, for the next steps. Reinforce their determination by contracts made within the group. Foresee, with them, the need to report back in Stage 31.

Keeping healthy – an attempt to take the topic from the level of information to responsibility for personal action and routines.

STAGE 31 *Spring Term*

PROGRAMME

Greetings and caring.

Action research with parents:
Progress reports on action taken. Further consideration of individual strategies. Reinforcement of contracts to take action.

Parents and the school:
Should we consider some kind of evening occasion when first year parents could share our experience and concerns?

Progress with school work:
A statement about individual progress in school, making use of the third self-assessment (**Working Paper 11**).

Consider the action required, especially some consultation with subject teachers during the last week of term.

Personal interests:
What are your interests and hobbies? Arrange for certain members of the group to tell us about their hobbies in Stage 32.

OBJECTIVES AND COMMENTS

Follow up the action research to encourage individual action.

Explore the possibility of an occasion to be shared with the parents of the form or of the first year. To be considered again next term.

A stocktaking after two terms' work, leading to consultation with other teaching staff and realistic objectives for next term. A copy of **Working Paper 11** will be needed for each pupil.

Focus on interesting activities, including some discussion about the use of the Easter holidays.

Some group members should be prepared for a short account of their interests to be given to the whole form in Stage 32.

STAGE 32   *Spring Term*

(Final stage before Easter break.)

PROGRAMME

Greetings.

Caring:
  Is there anyone who should be contacted before
  or during the Easter holiday?

Progress with school work:
  Report the consultation with teachers that has
  taken place and plan any further action. Individual
  members should be encouraged, in small
  support groups, to establish realistic personal
  objectives for next term. Can we support one
  another in trying to achieve these objectives?

Personal interests:
  Several members of the group explain and are
  questioned about their hobbies and interests.
  Engage the support of the group in helping
  individuals to develop these public statements.
  Small group discussion – what will you be doing
  during the Easter holidays?

Adieus and good wishes for the Easter break.

OBJECTIVES AND COMMENTS

A serious and considered statement about objectives
is required. Written objectives would be
helpful, – so that reference back can be made next
term.

Attempt to engage group support for individuals in
their objectives.

Stimulating and confirming personal interests.

Helping some young people in their attempts to
address the whole class.

PLANNING SCHEDULE: YEAR ONE

THEME	STAGE 33	STAGE 34	STAGE 35	STAGE 36	STAGE 37	STAGE 38
The pupil's place in the school		Our group— how are we doing?*	Organising a parents' evening.**	Parents' evening planning.**	Staging a parents' evening.***	Review of parents' evening**
Caring community	Review methods. Renew contracts.*					Review of caring routines*
Relationships, the self and social skills	Relationships with teachers.**	Teacher as a visitor.***	People in authority.***	People in authority— a visitor.***	Friendship —revision and individual support.**	Communication with parents.*
Communication skills						
School work and study skills	Revise third self-assessment— statement of objectives.**	Objectives—how can we support one another?*				
Academic guidance and careers education						
Health and hygiene						
Personal interests						Interests for half-term break.*

STAGE 33   *Summer Term*

(*First stage after Easter break*.)

PROGRAMME

Greetings:
  Welcome back. How was the Easter break? Renew contracts.

Review methods of caring, and possibly change the members of the caring group.

Progress with school work:
  Review the personal objectives established at the end of last term and consider how these are to be pursued.

Relationships with teachers:
  Role-play a series of school situations involving pupils and teachers, e.g. a teacher coping with a pupil who has been hurt; checking horseplay in the corridor; coping with pupils arriving after the class has begun; pupil referred to year or house head for cheeky behaviour.

  Question a visiting teacher about her day's work (prepare in small groups). Include questions like, 'What do you find most enjoyable?' 'What do you find most difficult?' The agenda should begin with personal issues as usual.

Prepare to receive another teacher as visitor in Stage 34.

OBJECTIVES AND COMMENTS

A special effort to bring the group together again, and to renew support and contracts.

A special review to set going the organisation of caring for the Summer term.

Setting a plan of individual action for the Summer term. This should be written if possible for later reference. Refer back to **Working Paper 11**.

Increasing the ease of contact between pupil and teacher, and in particular nurturing a sense of teacher-accessibility in the minds of the pupils.

Use the immediate contact with the form teacher as a point of departure.

Preparation for meeting another teacher as a visitor should include interest in both the person and his/her professional duties.

An exchange of teachers may be convenient – see notes in Stage 34.

STAGE 34 *Summer Term*

PROGRAMME

Greetings and caring.

How are we doing as a form?
Review of general behaviour in lessons and in moving around the school.

Relationships with teachers:
Receiving another teacher as a visitor:
(a) Revise agenda.
(b) Role-play reception and conclusion.

Receive the teacher as visitor.

(a) Review the performance of the group.
(b) Small group discussion – how can we ensure easy contact with our teachers?

Progress with school work:
Discussion in small support groups with open exchanges.

(a) Review objectives.
(b) How can we support one another in achieving these objectives?

Parents and school:
Look forward to parents' evening in Stage 37

OBJECTIVES AND COMMENTS

Review general behaviour patterns. Refer back to last term's discussions (Stages 27–9).

If necessary, conduct this session simultaneously in several classes and exchange the teachers.

Make this a frank and personal exchange, in which the teacher shares his dilemmas with the pupils.

The ways of easing communication between pupils and teachers should be an important issue both during the visit and in the discussion that follows.

Try to induce mutual support in attempting to reach individual work objectives.

Some preliminary discussion. Fix the date, but leave more detailed discussion until Stages 35 and 36.

STAGE 35

PROGRAMME

Greetings and caring.

Our parents and school:
We have been keeping our parents informed about our work in school. Could we invite them to a parents' evening for our tutorial group in Stage 37? What kind of evening should it be? (Brainstorming session in small groups for suggestions.) Who will help to organise the evening?
How will you invite your parents?
Role-play approaches.

People in authority:
Discussion in small groups and open exchanges.
E.g.
When my mother tells me what to do, I . . .
When my father tells me what to do, I . . .
When a teacher tells me what to do, I . . .
When I come across the headmaster in the school, I feel . . .

Role-play one or two of these situations.
What is it like to be the person who takes responsibility for telling other people what to do – especially if the other person is unwilling? Role-play a typical life situation suggested by the young people, and explore the position of the person in authority.

Prepare agenda for a visitor at Stage 36 – someone in authority in the school:
(a) To know the visitor as a person.
(b) To learn about what he/she has to do as a person in authority – including punishment.
(c) To explore with him/her how he/she feels about it all.

OBJECTIVES AND COMMENTS

Building up communication between parents and young people about school and between parents and the school.

Design the preparation and occasion to increase the young people's responsibility for events outside their own group meetings. The young people could include some of the exercises they have experienced in the pastoral work as part of the programme.

First take the young people into an awareness of their own feelings towards authority.

Then get them to explore the position of the person in authority.

The visitor will be chosen as being seen to exercise authority in the school, and the preparation to meet the visitor should have a bias towards that.

STAGE 36   *Summer Term*

PROGRAMME

Greetings and caring.

Our parents and the school:
  Finalise the form that the parents' evening will take. Decide how the occasion will be organised and allocate duties: e.g. programme, display, invitations, reception, entertainment and conclusion.

Looking at authority – receiving the visitor:
  (a) Revise agenda.
  (b) Role-play reception and conclusion.

  Receive the visitor.

  (a) What did we learn?
  (b) How well did we cope?

OBJECTIVES AND COMMENTS

Allocation of duties will need to be followed up to make sure things are moving forward. Teams are more likely to see things through than individuals by themselves.

The conversation with the visitor should begin with a personal exchange. The discussion about authority should give the visitor an opportunity to challenge the young people about their own feelings and attitudes towards authority.

STAGE 37   *Summer Term*

PROGRAMME

Greetings and caring.

Parents' evening:
  Final plans and preparation. Has each team carried through their plans? Reports. Revise arrangements for reception, entertainment and conclusion.
  Introducing one's parents to classmates and teacher.

Review of friendship:
  Has our friendship circle changed since we last looked at this subject? Have we all some special friends? Is there anyone who feels short of friends? With whom shall we spend the half-term break – shall we all have friends at hand?

OBJECTIVES AND COMMENTS

Keep as much of the responsibility in the hands of the young people as possible, – but with the active support of the teacher.

A brief check that everyone is feeling easy in their friendships.

The teacher and group may wish to study the changes that have taken place. A repeat of **Working Paper 4** would achieve this.

STAGE 38   *Summer Term*

(Final stage before half-term break.)

PROGRAMME

Greetings and caring.

Parents' evening – report and review:
  (a) Report from each of the teams responsible for the occasion.
  (b) Comments about the effectiveness of each item in the programme.
  (c) Lessons for any similar occasion.
  (d) The impact of the evening on communication at home.

The half-term break:
  (a) How will you use your time – any ideas about interesting things to do?
  (b) Any arrangements for members of the group to meet during the holidays?

Adieus and good wishes.

OBJECTIVES AND COMMENTS

Review of routines and arrangements.

An opportunity for the young people to consider their success and difficulties in organising the event.

Consider any impact that the evening had upon the communication between parents and young people, and how this might be followed up.

Another opportunity to consider personal interests.

PLANNING SCHEDULE: YEAR ONE

THEME	STAGE 39	STAGE 40	STAGE 41	STAGE 42	STAGE 43	STAGE 44
The pupil's place in the school					Looking forward to being a second-year pupil. *	
Caring community	Review methods.*	Renew support.**				Good wishes. Arrangements for holiday contacts.*
Relationships, the self and social skills	The way we influence one another.***	Self-description —social skills.***	Personal objectives and mutual help.***	Social skills workshop.***	Social skills —visitors.***	
Communication skills				Communication skills.*	Practising speaking to the whole class—summer holidays. *	
School work and study skills	Revive statement of objectives. *					
Academic guidance and careers education						
Health and hygiene			Light evenings and hot weather.**			
Personal interests				Preparing to use summer holidays.*	Use of summer holidays. *	

STAGE 39

Summer Term

(*First stage after half-term break.*)

PROGRAMME

Greetings.

Revise methods of caring for the remainder of the Summer term.

Progress with school work:
Review and revise objectives. Consider personal strategies in small groups.

The ways we influence one another:
Explore the expectations that surround us by using **Working Paper 15**. Work through Socratic group discussion. Are the ways that we expect one another to behave always helpful? Can we think of any that we would like to change?

OBJECTIVES AND COMMENTS

An emphasis on revised objectives, planning strategies, and group support for the individual. Refer back to objectives established earlier in the term (Stages 33 and 34).

A simple exploration of group norms. **Working Paper 15** should serve as a useful introduction, but the teacher may be aware of obvious group controls operating in the classroom, which could serve as a focus for discussion, especially if there is a need to modify the behaviour. Discussion and decision about any changes that the group feels should take place.

STAGE 40

Summer Term

PROGRAMME

Greetings and caring.

Renew support:
Rocking in threes. Contracts in readiness for self-description.

Self-description – social skills:
Explore individual progress in social skills by using **Working Paper 13**. Encourage the pupils to work in small groups, especially to help one another to decide the points of progress they would like to make. Look forward to a declaration of personal objectives in Stage 41 and social skills workshops in Stages 42 and 43.

OBJECTIVES AND COMMENTS

Lift the level of support in readiness for the self-description. Pupils need to be able to be honest with themselves and with one another.

Set a serious tone, and encourage mutual support and help in determining individual positions.

Lead to an acknowledgment of any movement that has taken place, and to an optimism that further movement is possible.

What form will the social skills workshop take, and can the young people help to plan it?

A copy of **Working Paper 13** will be required for each pupil.

STAGE 41

PROGRAMME

Greetings and caring.

Social skills – personal objectives:
  (a) Review the self-description of Stage 40.
  (b) In small groups, review and crystallize individual objectives.
  (c) Open exchanges in the total group about personal objectives.

Helping individuals, and individuals helping themselves:
  (a) Difficulties in meeting people:
      What kinds of people? Role-play a meeting and greeting; make contracts to try this out as fieldwork. Can we offer any support in this?
  (b) Difficulties in conversation:
      Plan a conversation as fieldwork; work out agendas.
  (c) Shyness:
      Use the small group experimentally. Role-play some of the situations that are most difficult. Fieldwork assignment: what help can we offer? We must be careful that we do not deprive our shy friend of experience by answering for him/her.

Social skills workshop:
  Some preliminary planning.

Keeping healthy:
  Light evenings and warm weather – do we need to take special care? Cleanliness and hygiene. Exercise – including outdoor pursuits. Rest and sleep. Food.

OBJECTIVES AND COMMENTS

Use small groups to tease out statements of personal objectives.

Encourage public statements of those who are ready.

Work through small groups to allow individuals to prepare their approaches.

It may be inadvisable to collect together people with the same objectives, since they may not be able to help one another. This is especially true of the shy members.

The small groups should be able to plan most of their own activities. Open exchanges between the small groups about the way they are approaching this could be helpful.

Fieldwork – individual young people decide to try something outside the group meeting. Some may support others in doing this. Clear contracts will be required about the fieldwork to be attempted.

Look forward to Stages 42 and 43 to be ready for this preliminary planning. Will you be able to find sufficient visitors? (See **Working Paper 14.**)

Building upon previous conversations, with a change of emphasis.

STAGE 42

PROGRAMME

Greetings and caring.

Social skills – achieving personal objectives:
  (a) Update personal objectives.
  (b) Statement of strategies.

Social skills workshop – see **Working Paper 14**.
Prepare to receive visitors in Stage 43.

Preparing to use the Summer holidays:
  What are your plans? Will you be ready to tell the
  class about them in Stages 43 and 44?

OBJECTIVES AND COMMENTS

Encourage the young people to take their own
development seriously.

An active session involving each young person in
increasing his own level of competence. **Working
Paper 14** needs thought and adaptation as preparation for the session.

Leading to some thought about:
  (a) the creative use of the Summer holidays;
  (b) topics that can serve as a vehicle for individual statements to the whole group.

STAGE 43

Summer Term

PROGRAMME

Greetings and caring.

Social skills:
Review of objectives – meeting people, conversations, listening, speaking to larger groups.

Visitors:
(a) Revise agendas for initiating conversations.
(b) Role-play reception and conclusion.

Receive visitors in small groups, and conclude the visit. Review group and individual progress.

Social skills workshop:
Continue any unfinished business.

Plans for the Summer holidays – statements to the whole group:
(a) Who is ready to speak to the whole group?
(b) Rehearsal in small groups.
(c) Statements to the whole group.
(d) More required for next time.

Looking forward to being second year pupils:
How can we be helpful to next year's first year pupils? (Discussion in small groups.) How did you feel when you first joined this school? Use **Working Paper 3**.

OBJECTIVES AND COMMENTS

Reminder and renewal of contracts.

Sharing with visitors the kind of experience that the group has been having, and as practice for members of the group who are steadily increasing their skills. A genuine interest in the visitor as a person should serve as the focus of the exchange.

Repeat any exercises that there is time for.

An exchange of ideas may inspire others to follow additional interests, and could lead to combined action by several members of the group. This will be an important experience in making a public statement for some members of the group.

Engaging the group to think responsibly about their position next term. If next year's first year pupils are to visit the school, the present first year might share the responsibility for receiving them. Use the enquiry **Working Paper 3**.
(a) as a way of interesting the young people in caring for next year's first year pupils;
(b) as information for the school in preparing for next year's intake.

STAGE 44   *Summer Term*

(Final stage of first year)

PROGRAMME

Greetings and caring:
    Is anybody in difficulties that will affect the
    summer holidays?

Being second year pupils:
    What do we need to know about next term, e.g.
    date of return, form room, the kind of
    programme? How can we be helpful to next
    year's pupils?

    (a) Revise discussion in small groups.
    (b) Open exchanges.

The Summer holidays – statements to the whole
group:
    (a) Who will tell us about plans or interests?
    (b) Rehearsal in small groups.
    (c) Speaking to the whole group.

Farewells:
    Are there any arrangements for meeting during
    the holidays? Adieus and good wishes for the
    holiday.

OBJECTIVES AND COMMENTS

Make sure that anyone in difficulty is remembered.
    Arrangements may be needed for visits after
    school has finished.

This will need to be picked up at the beginning of
    next term, so that the new first years will feel the
    support of these older pupils.

Encourage some of the more timid to make an
    attempt at speaking to the whole group. Make
    sure that their efforts are *seen* to be appreciated.

Some cooperative action may encourage several of
    the more timid pupils to venture.

WORKING PAPERS FOR THE FIRST YEAR PROGRAMME

WORKING PAPER 1

First year pupils finding their way around the school

1   True to the spirit of the whole of this programme, the first year pupils should be helped to find their own way around the school rather than to be conducted from place to place.

2   But this should be done in a controlled manner, building the confidence of the young people and ensuring responsible behaviour.

3   An early objective should be for them to become familiar with the route to certain base points in the school, from which subsequent directions can begin.

4   One of the methods might be to arrange a school navigation exercise – a cross between a treasure hunt and an orienteering exercise.
    (a) Sketch plans will be prepared, together with a schedule of places to be found by small parties of young people. Directions will include the customary modes of movement along corridors and stairs.
    (b) The emphasis will be on young people finding their way by their own orienteering, rather than following a senior.
    (c) Older pupils, e.g. sixth formers or even second formers, who may already have met the young people concerned, will be stationed at strategic places. In this way it will be possible to ensure that the small groups of first formers are never out of sight of someone who could help them.
    (d) Groups of, say, five or six pupils, equipped with sketch plans and schedules, will travel together, and will be required to obtain the signature of the people stationed at the places to which their schedules direct them.

5   It is assumed that before this happens, there will have been a preparatory programme designed to create a supportive situation in each pastoral group.

WORKING PAPER 2

Our responsibilities in school

Agenda for discussion in small groups with open exchanges.

1 Do we know what is expected of us in walking along the corridors?
   And on the stairs?

2 Do we arrive on time and in good order at assemblies?
   How do we feel about the assemblies?

3 Are we satisfied with what happens at dinner time?

4 Is everything in good order at break time?

5 What about the way we dress – is it right and tidy?

6 Can you think of anything that is especially helpful or praiseworthy about
   our form?

7 Have we a good understanding with our teachers?

8 Have any of our group been getting into trouble?
   Could we all help in any way?

9 Is there anything we do as a whole form that should be improved?

WORKING PAPER 3

When we first joined the school

1   When you first came into the school, which door did you arrive by?

2   Were you clear about where you should go?

3   Who was the first teacher you met – can you remember?
     What happened?

4   Can you remember which classroom you first went into?
     How did you get there?

5   Were your first few minutes in the school:
     exciting?
     frightening?
     reassuring?

6   How did you find out where the toilets were?

7   How did you find your way to the next classroom?
     Where was it?

8   How did you find your way to the gym?

9   What about the preparation for gym – did you know where the changing
     rooms were and what to do?

     How did you find out?

10   How did you find your way:
     (a) to the science laboratories?
     (b) to the art and craft rooms?
     (c) to the woodwork/metalwork room?
     (d) to the domestic science rooms?

11 How did you learn how you are expected to move around the school – for example, behaviour in corridors?

and which stairs to use?

12 When and how did you learn where the office was?

And what to do when you went to the office?

13 At what stage did you learn about looking after your own property?

And how did you learn about this?

14 Did you know what to do if you lost any of your property?

How did you find out?

15 Were you ever confused?

What caused this?

16 Were you ever lost?

Where were you lost and where were you going?

What did you do about it?

17 Have you any suggestions to make that would help next year's first year pupils to find their way about the school more easily?

WORKING PAPER 4

Who are my friends?

Name .... Form ....

Have you any special friends? Who are they?

Name ....

How long have you been friends?

When did you first meet?

Where did you first meet?

Is this friend in this school?

Is this friend in this form?

Where do you meet now?

What do you do together?

Name ....

How long have you been friends?

When did you first meet?

Where did you first meet?

Is this friend in this school?

Is this friend in this form?

Where do you meet now?

What do you do together?

Name ....

How long have you been friends?

When did you first meet?

Where did you first meet?

Is this friend in this school?

Is this friend in this form?

Where do you meet now?

What do you do together?

Name ....

How long have you been friends?

When did you first meet?

Where did you first meet?

Is this friend in this school?

Is this friend in this form?

Where do you meet now?

What do you do together?

Name ....

How long have you been friends?

When did you first meet?

Where did you first meet?

Is this friend in this school?

Is this friend in this form?

Where do you meet now?

What do you do together?

WORKING PAPER 5

Getting on with other boys and girls of our own age

Do you remember we talked before about our *special* friends?
    Have these changed?
    Who are they now?

Have you other friends you go around with?
    Who are they?

    Where do you meet?

    What do you do together?

Are there other people of your own age that you have to get on with?
Do you come across them in a particular place?
    The people you meet.   Where you meet them.

Do you like meeting all these people?
    Some I like because . . .

    Some I don't like because . . .

How do you think that your friends would describe you?

How would the people you don't like describe you?

How do you behave to the people you don't like?

WORKING PAPER 6

Conversations between girls and boys: how we see life

An agenda for use in small group discussions with open exchanges. *Mixed* groups of threes and fours.

1   What makes you laugh?

2   What makes you sad?

3   When you have had a good day – what will have happened?

4   When you have had a bad day – what will have happened?

5   'When I am with my friends, we . . .'

6   'When I am at home with my parents, I . . .'

7   'By next year I would like to . . .'

8   'By the time I'm twenty I should think I . . .'

9   'I am frightened by . . .'

10   'I am most confident when . . .'

11   'My greatest interests are . . .'

WORKING PAPER 7

Action research into the position of our parents as we are growing up

How did it feel to you when I changed from junior to senior school?

Was it very different from your feelings when I first started school?

Can you remember what it felt like when you began senior school?
– were you excited?
– can you remember being anxious? What about?
– how did you find senior school when you began?

When you were my age:
– what were the good things in life?
– what were you interested in?
– were you ever shocked, disturbed or embarrassed by anything?

What do you feel about my life at school?
– do you feel that you know about it?
– do you ever feel left out?

Do you feel the relationships between us have changed since I have been going to senior school?

Is this natural and good or do you feel that it is in some ways **unhelpful**?

We are thinking of arranging a parents' evening next term. **Would you be** interested in coming along?

WORKING PAPER 8

Progress with lessons – First self-assessment

Name . . . . Form . . . .

1   During lessons I like it when . . . . .

2   I do not like it when . . . . .

3   I get really worried when . . . . .

4   I was frightened when . . . . .

5   I feel that I am getting on well in the following lessons:

6   I feel that I am falling behind in the following lessons:

Summary

I would like to do better in lessons in the following ways:

1

2

WORKING PAPER 9

Progress with lessons – Second self-assessment

Name .... Form ....

1   Do you always understand what the teacher says in class?

2   Do you sometimes not understand what the teacher writes on the board?

3   Can you write easily and neatly or is writing difficult?

4   When you write notes in your book, is it easy – difficult – just all right?

5   Can you work out the arithmetic examples?

6   How do you get on with your spelling?

7   How do you get on with writing essays?

8   Do you have difficulty with drawing, e.g. maps, illustrations?

9   Do you make contributions to discussions in class or do you find this difficult?

Summary

Are there any of these things you would like to do better – in order of importance?

1

2

3

WORKING PAPER 10

Coping with difficulties in school work

An agenda for small group discussion with open exchanges, in preparation for a conversation with a senior member of staff as a visitor.

1   Have you found some of the subjects new and difficult?

2   Are you able to ask questions of the teacher when there is something that you do not understand?

3   If you need help with a problem associated with your school work whom should you approach and how should you ask for it?

4   Have you met difficulties with any skills that enter a number of subjects, e.g. writing, spelling, drawing diagrams, doing calculations, putting a framework of ideas together?

5   What is the best way of helping one another?

6   Homework – do you have difficulty:
    (a) in finding a space where you can do homework?
    (b) in getting well organised?
    (c) in getting down to it?

WORKING PAPER 11

Progress with lessons – Third self-assessment

Name .... Form ....

1 I feel that I am making satisfactory progress in . . .

2 I enjoy, but I am not so good at . . .

3 I feel that I am falling behind with . . .

4 I do not like . . .

5 I enjoy .... but
I have difficulty in working out . . .

6 I find it difficult to understand . . .

7 I find writing . . .

8 I am .... at getting down to my
homework.

These are the ways in which I would most like to improve my school work:

1

2

3

WORKING PAPER 12

Growing up – how are you finding it?

1   When you moved from junior to senior school:
    (a) There were a lot more people to cope with – how did you find it?
    (b) Have your friends changed at all?
    (c) Have you felt uncertain?
    (d) Are you ever shy?

2   At home:
    (a) As you have become older, has it changed your position at home?
    (b) Do your parents expect anything different from you?

3   Our bodies:
    (a) As you have become bigger, have your arms and legs worked in the
        same way?
    (b) Do you like your shape?
    (c) Do you like your looks?
    (d) Have you noticed other changes in yourself?
    (e) Have you been anxious about not knowing things about yourself?

4   You are beginning to be aware of more things around you.
    (a) Have there been things that have disturbed you or made you curious?
    (b) Has anybody disturbed you by what he/she
        – has said to you?
        – has done to you?

5   We shall be receiving a visitor who knows a lot about boys and girls
    growing up.
    Is there anything you would like to know?

WORKING PAPER 13

Social skills: a progress report

Name .... Group ....

1 Read each statement and decide whether it is very much like you, not at all like you, or somewhere in between. Indicate where you think you are with a tick.

2 When you have been through them all, think back to how you were last September when you first came to this school. Mark where you think you were then with an X.

3 Where would you like to be? Indicate this with △.

4 When you have finished all this, decide what you would most like to change. Write this at the end of the paper in order of importance 1 to 3.

	Very much like me	Like me	Neutral	Not like me	Not at all like me
Meeting and greeting people:					
1 I can meet and greet people of my own age very easily.					
2 I find it difficult to meet boys/girls (opposite).					
3 I am at ease when meeting adults whom I already know.					
4 I am very shy.					

	Very much like me	Like me	Neutral	Not like me	Not at all like me
Conversations:					
5 I can chat easily with my friends.					
6 It is difficult to talk with people of my own age whom I don't know well.					
7 I am confused and stuck for words when a teacher or any other adult asks me a question.					
8 I can usually hold an interesting conversation with someone I meet.					
9 I am a good listener.					
10 I find it easy to talk in front of the whole class.					

I would like it to be easier to do the following:

1

2

3

WORKING PAPER 14

Social skills workshop

An active session of action and planning, breaking rapidly from small groups to whole group, and back to small groups as required.

1 Meeting and greeting.
   (a) Small group discussion – whom do you find it difficult to meet? Open exchange.
   (b) Role-play situations that would involve the kinds of people named.
       (i) An example in the whole group.
       (ii) Decision in small groups about the kinds of situations to be enacted. Open exchange.
       (iii) Small groups to role-play the situations that have been identified – engaging especially the young people who feel that they need practice in that situation.
       (iv) Special care for the shy people – give them time and space.

2 Eye contact – how easily can we meet other people's eyes?
   (a) Move around the room, taking both the hands of the other people in the group, and engaging them in momentary eye contact.
   (b) Try it again, but hold the eye contact just a little longer.
   (c) Has it become easier? Does anybody find it very difficult? Can they practice it for themselves? Could we all help and encourage?

3 Practising conversation – working in small groups.
   (a) Do we find it difficult to begin a conversation. With what kind of person? Open exchange.
   (b) Some quick thinking about suitable agendas for a conversation.
   (c) Role-play beginning a conversation. Those who want the practice to take the initiative. Take turns in small groups.
   (d) Can we practise this as fieldwork? With whom? Open statements about intentions. Agreements to report experience at next meeting.

4 Could we suggest a number of visitors for the next meeting – e.g. senior citizens, sixth formers, parents, neighbours – one for each small group (of as few as two or three if possible).
   (a) What should the conversations be about?
       How should we prepare ourselves to be interested in the visitors?

(b) Who will do what? Give opportunities for the shy people to try anything that they feel they could manage.

(c) Who will invite whom, and arrange for them to arrive and be received?

WORKING PAPER 15

The way we influence one another

Proceed through Socratic group discussion. The prompts should serve to create
an awareness of the way group members influence one another, but the teacher
should not hesitate to substitute questions about obvious group norms that
actually exist in the classroom and elsewhere.

Expected behaviour amongst friends
Why do we not let our friends down?
How would they feel if you were to do so?
What would they say or do to you?

Fashion and dress
Have you noticed how groups of people wear similar clothes?
How would you feel if you found that you were wearing a different kind of
clothes from the rest of your group?
Is it possible that other people might make fun of us?

Breaking a custom
Do any of us call for one another on the way to school?
How would we feel if our friend stopped calling for us?
Would you think that you may have done something wrong?
Could it be a way of punishing us?
Are there other customs you feel that you are required to follow?

Other people's expectations
So do we tend to feel that we should do what people expect of us?
Do we feel that they may criticise us if we don't?

Are you expected to do certain things at home?
What would happen if you did not do those things?

Do you expect your parents to do certain things?
What kind of things?
How would you react if they were not to do those things?

In the classroom

In the classroom, my classmates would expect me to . . . . .

Some of my classmates would be cross if I were to . . . . .

THE SECOND YEAR PROGRAMME

INTRODUCTION

A programme for second year pupils needs to have its own points of emphasis. The school is no longer new to them as it was at the beginning of the first year; they are past the stage of needing the special attention given in the induction programme, but they have not yet reached the stage of decision, either about the subjects to be followed for examinations or the more distant prospect of choosing a career. There is a danger of the pupils feeling 'in between'. They are already familiar with the school routines, but they could feel that they have no special place in the school.

In this programme, some attention is given to the growing responsibility of the pastoral group for the care of their own members. The young people are encouraged to develop their study skills and social skills. The programme is more outward looking, inviting the young people to consider their relationships with their parents and with other adults, and their responsibilities in the wider community. It is also designed to maintain their commitment to the school. For example, it is suggested that they should share the responsibility for certain second year events.

TIMETABLE

This programme is planned in thirty-six stages, six for each half-term. It is assumed that a weekly period of not less than thirty-five minutes will be devoted to pastoral work, together with, say, two or three registration times each week. As long as there is an undisturbed period each week devoted to the work, it will be possible to use any shorter periods at other times to follow up the activities already initiated. There would be enough material in this programme to occupy an hour-long period each week. There is an associated set of working papers to accompany the programme.

The school's special points of emphasis or interest can be added to the programme at appropriate stages.

CONTINUITY

It is assumed that the young people for whom this programme has been designed will have experienced the first year programme that forms part of this series. If, on the other hand, the young people are being introduced newly to this programme at the second year, then some of the early material from the first year programme should be included. It is especially important that the early first year exercises to establish a supportive group should be included, together with the skills of conversation and listening.

Broad themes run through all the programmes as indicated by the planning schedules that precede each half-term's work. The programme is arranged in rounded half-term sequences, but there is also considerable carry-over from one half-term to the next. The weighting that is given to any one item on the schedules is indicated by one to three asterisks.

SEQUENCE AND REINFORCEMENT

There is a strong sequence in the sense that each stage assumes the experience embodied in the previous stages, and in turn serves as a foundation for the experiences that follow. Unless a sequence is maintained, much of the impact of the work could be lost. Most of the activities serve several purposes at once. This is indicated in the comments that accompany each stage, but it is only by looking forward that the tutor will be able to see the interlocking nature of the steps, and to capitalise on the reinforcement inherent in the programme.

THE PROGRAMMES AND WORKING PAPERS

The programme for each stage is laid out in the left-hand column, with objectives and suggestions for the tutor in the right-hand column. The programmes are supported by a set of pastoral Working Papers (to be found between pages 149 and 178) and references to these are by numbers in the text.

The use of the symbol ● indicates that a copy of the Working Paper is needed for each pupil.

PLANNING SCHEDULE: YEAR TWO

THEME	STAGE 1	STAGE 2	STAGE 3	STAGE 4	STAGE 5	STAGE 6
The pupil's place in the school	Responsibilities as second-year pupils. Concern for first-year pupils.*	Being second-year pupils—preparing conversation with pastoral head.*	Pastoral head as visitor.***		Review of group behaviour.*	
Caring community	Greetings and new contracts. Shared responsibility for caring.**	Settle routine for caring. Renew support.**		Review caring routine.		Sharing the administration —review of routines.**
Relationships, the self and social skills	Coping with people we do not know.*					
Communication skills		Personal conversations. Prepare for conversations outside the group.**	Report conversations. Sustained conversations with peers.*	Report outside conversations with adults.*	Report outside conversations. Revise agendas.*	
School work and study skills	Check lesson and homework programme.*		About homework routines —diary.*	Enquiry about homework routines —report.**	Review of homework methods.***	Homework, Learning how to help one another.**
Personal interests	Mutual enquiries about summer holidays.*					Using our leisure. Some ideas for the programme.*

STAGE 1   *Autumn Term*

(First stage of second year.)

PROGRAMME

Greetings:
Welcome back. Is anyone new this term? Renew contracts and support.

Summer holidays:
Is there anything interesting to tell one another? Discussion in small groups and open exchanges.

Now we are second year pupils:
Initiate small group discussion and open exchanges. What changes does this new year mean in position and responsibilities? Could we offer support to first year pupils? How do we begin a conversation with someone we don't know? Role-play the approach.

Caring:
Could we take more of the responsibility this year? How should this be approached? Small groups to discuss and make suggestions. Return suggestions to the small groups and lead to corporate decisions.

Lessons and homework:
Check lesson and homework timetable.

OBJECTIVES AND COMMENTS

Proceed through several distinct steps. Leave sufficient time for general greetings. Special care for any newcomers. Revive idea of contracts for mutual caring and support.

Emphasis on the extension of experience.

Being a second year pupil – introduction to discussion in Stages 2 and 3.
Encourage supportive attitude to first year pupils. Conversation with unfamiliar person is the first step in a more outward-looking programme this year.

Encourage group to take major responsibility for the caring routine – *their* group – absences, sickness, general well-being, and coping with trouble in school as far as possible.

Make sure that everyone is settled.

STAGE 2

PROGRAMME

Greetings.

Focus on trust and support:
  Trust walk with someone you have not done this with before. Be inventive. Make it a special and interesting experience.

Caring:
  Settle the routine and the people who are to lead it.

Personal conversations:
  (a) Agendas – developing agendas for sustained personal conversation. Small group discussions leading to open exchanges.
  (b) Conversations in twos leading to introducing partners in fours – as a colour or a flower.
  (c) Try further conversations with people of your own age outside the group. Who will this be? Settle contracts in small groups. Role-play approaches.

Being a second year pupil:
  Prepare agenda for a conversation with a senior member of staff in Stage 3:
  (a) a personal conversation with the visitor;
  (b) the kind of school programme planned for the second year;
  (c) the special things we should be watching for;
  (d) the ways in which we could be helpful to the first year pupils.

OBJECTIVES AND COMMENTS

Regenerate trust and support. Inspire inventiveness. Encourage mixed pairs in preparation for discussions between boys and girls later this term.

The extension of agendas will serve as a basis for further work later this term.

Try to gain an acceptance of outside conversations as a means of extending conversation skills.

Make sure that the personal side of the conversation receives attention.

Try to ensure that there is a *conversation* about being a second year pupil – avoid a catalogue of staff expectations.

STAGE 3

PROGRAMME

Greetings and caring.

Report conversations outside the group: Report to small groups, leading to open exchanges; role-play as appropriate. Can we manage a sustained conversation? Try a conversation with an adult. Revise agenda, role-play. Renew contracts, to report back in Stage 4.

Being a second year pupil – member of senior staff as visitor:
(a) Revise agenda.
(b) Role-play reception and conclusion.

Receive the visitor.

(a) What have we learnt?
(b) How well did we cope?

Homework:
Prepare for an enquiry about homework methods and routine using **Working Paper 27**. Look through the enquiry in small groups, with the tutor moving the discussion on step-by-step. How can you interest your parents in the enquiry? Bring the completed enquiry to Stage 4.

OBJECTIVES AND COMMENTS

Encourage the pupils to accept the value of practising conversation skills. In revising agenda, attempt also to deepen and extend. Determination and real contracts may be required to ensure that fieldwork is attempted. Small group support is important.

See that the initiative is with the young people, although the visitor will also have his own messages to get over. A careful briefing with the visitor before the visit will help you to ensure that the preparation is appropriate.

Although the main purpose is to help the young person to look into his/her own programme and approaches, the enquiry will also help the school to review the general arrangements for homework. A copy of **Working Paper 27** will be required for each pupil. This is an opportunity to involve parents also. The tutor will need to see the completed working papers.

STAGE 4   *Autumn Term*

PROGRAMME

Greetings.

Review caring routine.

Report back outside conversation with adult:
Extend practice with outside conversations in
readiness for a review of skills and framework in
Stage 5.

Enquiry into homework programme: Work
through small groups with open exchanges
(**Working Paper 27**).
  (a) Timetable:
    (i) At what time of the evening or weekend
      did you do your homework? And was
      this consistent?
    (ii) How do you decide when to do it? Do
      you decide or just drift?
    (iii) Did your homework tend to hang over
      your head for most of the evening?
  (b) Planning:
    (i) Would it be advisable to plan a time-
      table so that you can feel free outside
      those times?
    (ii) How can you make sure that you keep
      to your timetable?
    (iii) Plan a timetable in discussion with your
      small group.
  (c) Experiment with your timetable this week.
  We will discuss your experiment and the
  remainder of the enquiry in Stage 5.

OBJECTIVES AND COMMENTS

Leave serious discussions of agendas until Stage 5.
Encourage extended practice in outside conversations.

Focus on planning a timetable, and ways of setting
targets and sticking to them.

Leave the remainder of the enquiry until Stage 5.

Encourage firm contracts to carry through a timetable experiment and report back in Stage 5.

Keep in mind the value of this enquiry to the school
as well as to the young people – are there any
matters to raise in staff consultation?

STAGE 5   *Autumn Term*

PROGRAMME

Greetings and caring.

Homework – working through small groups and open exchanges:

(a) Timetable – how did your experiment work out?

(i) Was your suggested timing suitable?

(ii) Were you able to keep to your plans? How did you remind yourself?

(iii) Do your plans need any amendment? Recast your plans and put them into action.

(b) Conditions of work:

(i) Do you have to work with other people in the room?

(ii) Do you need to work out special strategies to cope with this?

(iii) Do you find television or radio a distraction? Could any kind of rearrangement help?

(c) Feelings about homework:

(i) Did you find any of your homework especially   enjoyable – unpleasant – easy – difficult?

(ii) Is there anything you need to discuss with the subject teacher?

(iii) Is there anything you could do to help yourself?

(iv) Are there any special anxieties (question 4 of the enquiry)?

(d) Have you shared this discussion with your parents? Can they support you in your planning?

Outside conversations:

Report in small groups with open exchanges. Role-play where appropriate.

Agendas and frameworks:

We need to be able to construct agendas and frameworks quickly for all kinds of purposes – conversations, essays, letters, enquiries, answers to examination questions. So let us build on our recent experience by quickly reconstructing a framework for a conversation with a friendly adult. Work through small groups, reporting to the whole group. First suggest broad headings –

OBJECTIVES AND COMMENTS

Process pupils' experience in trying a timetable and lead on to suitable amendments.

Encourage them to consider ways of helping themselves to measure up to their good intentions.

We all tend to fit into the situation to which we are accustomed. You may need to induce an interest in the possibility even of minor rearrangements of physical conditions.

The teachers responsible for setting the homework would be interested in this part of the enquiry. A number of young people may need some simple assistance that they are too timid to ask for.

It is vital that parents should have shared this enquiry.

The young people should by this time be approaching outside conversations with greater ease.

The rapid structuring of frameworks is an important skill in life in general as well as in school. It is largely a matter of seeing the broad issues or principles involved, and how these could be developed. The ability to analyse material and arguments has similar roots. (See also Stage 7.) Some quick-fire experience at this stage will prepare for later work. Try to get some urgency into the exercise.

PROGRAMME

areas of life that might provide a focus. Now each group take one of those broad headings and suggest several sub-headings that would serve to explore that area. We shall be doing more with this in Stage 7.

Review of the group's behaviour:
A discussion of the group's general behaviour in the school. A framework for discussion is given in **Working Paper 16**. Work through small group discussion and open exchanges.

OBJECTIVES AND COMMENTS

Both helpful and unhelpful group norms may have been built up.
The group may wish to strengthen some and to modify others.

STAGE 6

Autumn Term

(*Last stage before half-term break*.)

PROGRAMME

Greetings.

Caring and administration:
How far could members of the group share the essential administration?

(a) A description of the administration that must be accomplished in an explanation/question session.
(b) Small group discussion – how much of this could be taken over by the members of the group.
(c) How would it be organised?
(d) Make arrangements that will be tried after the half-term break.

Approaches to homework:
Review progress in small groups with open exchanges.

(a) Planning and keeping to a timetable.
(b) Making the best of the conditions of work at home.
(c) Getting on top of the material – consultation with subject teachers.

Helping one another with school work:
Small group discussion and open exchanges.

(a) Are there ways in which we can help one another with our school work?
(b) Does this happen already – and if so how is it being done?
(c) It is no help to the other person if we save him/her the effort. So how can we help without actually doing the work?

The use of leisure:
How do we or could we use our leisure? Let us have some ideas about the kinds of things we might look at in this year's group programme. And what about the half-term holiday?

OBJECTIVES AND COMMENTS

With the several objectives of

(a) relieving the form teacher of routines that deflect him from work with the pupils;
(b) providing young people with experience of administrative functions;
(c) increasing a sense that the well-being of the group is the responsibility of its members.

Some preparatory staff discussion and study will be required in order to identify any functions that might be shared with the young people.

Consolidate the discussion and progress.
Pay special attention to:
adaptation of physical conditions; sticking to a timetable; engaging the interest and support of parents; consultation with subject teachers.

Pupils often help their friends – but not always to their advantage.

Cooperation in learning can be enjoyable and creative, but only when the participants have learnt how to help one another to learn.

There are spaces for this later in the programme – and ideas would be helpful. You are also focusing on the use of the half-term holiday.

PLANNING SCHEDULE: YEAR TWO

THEME	STAGE 7	STAGE 8	STAGE 9	STAGE 10	STAGE 11	STAGE 12
The pupil's place in the school	How do we find school?**	How do we find school? Second-year Christmas event. Year meeting.**	Christmas event —report from representatives.*	Christmas event —the group's contribution.*	Christmas event —rehearse group's contribution.**	Taking responsibility for an assembly next term.**
Caring community	Extend caring to include sharing administration.*	Consolidate caring/administration.*			Trust walk, boys and girls.*	Review method of caring/administration.*
Relationships, the self and social skills			What kind of friend am I?**	Personal responsibilities in friendship.*	Boys and girls —the way they see life.**	Boys and girls —sharing activities; —concern for one another.**
Communication skills	Public statements.	Presentation of frameworks.**		Reporting school experience with parents.*		
School work and study skills	{ Agendas and frameworks.**			Fourth self-assessment.**	Statement of personal objectives.*	
Academic guidance and careers education						
Health and hygiene						
Personal interests						

STAGE 7

(*First stage after half-term break.*)

PROGRAMME

Greetings.

Caring and administration:
Set new arrangements in motion, especially for sharing the administration.

How do we find school?
Small group discussion with open exchanges, using **Working Paper 28** as an agenda.

Agendas and frameworks.
Practice in the rapid formulation of agendas and frameworks.
First choose a subject and then through small group discussion and open exchanges:
Throw up main headings, and settle these through open exchanges. Then allocate a heading to each group, who will producc relevant sub-headings. Each group to submit their findings to the critical attention of the whole group.
Possible topics could be related to the discussion about school – the preparation of very short statements about specific aspects under discussion.
E.g. What school means to me
If I were a teacher
A letter to my headmaster
'Mr Chairman and fellow councillors – these are the most important things to consider when setting up our schools.'

OBJECTIVES AND COMMENTS

Open and frank exchanges are essential. Use the discussion as much to inform the school as to influence the young people. Use **Working Paper 28** as a framework for discussion, *not* as a work sheet.

This follows on from Stage 5. Get some urgency into the work: a brief period in small groups and a rapid exchange of ideas – brainstorming.

An approach to the basic skills of creating frameworks for essays, talks, letters, examination answers, agendas for conversations. Make sure the young people grasp the relevance of the exercise.

This session leads, in Stage 8, to members of the group presenting their subject in, say, two-minute public statements to the whole group.

It is suggested that there should be a representative year meeting at which views produced by the discussion on 'How do we find school?' are submitted to the year staff.

The second year meeting might take the form of a working party including all the second year form teachers and several representatives from each form. Detailed discussion could be conducted through small groups reporting to the whole meeting. The working party would be seen as an advisory body.

STAGE 8

PROGRAMME

Greetings and caring:
  Consolidate new arrangements for caring and administration.

Year meetings:
  Arrangements for a meeting of representatives of each form in the second year to discuss:

  (a) The 'How do we find school?' enquiry.
  (b) Plans for a Christmas event for year two.

How do we find school?
  (a) The main issues arising from previous discussion;
  (b) Frameworks and agendas – prepare very brief statements putting forward these main issues. (Suitable for the year meeting.) Work through small groups.

Second year Christmas event:
  (a) What kind of event should this be?
  (b) What kind of contribution to the programme would our form like to make?
  (c) Framework and agendas – prepare very brief statements putting forward these ideas.

Representatives to second year meeting:
  (a) Who will speak for us?
  (b) What is their function?
  (c) How will they report back to us?
  (d) Help the appointed representatives to rehearse their contribution to the meeting.

OBJECTIVES AND COMMENTS

The purpose and organisation of a year meeting will need to be considered before any of the preparatory discussions begin.

Formulate the main findings arising out of the previous discussion and prepare to make statements to the second year meeting.

Use the occasion as an opportunity to develop skills in the rapid development of frameworks and agendas, and in making public statements.

A feasibility study by the year staff should have preceded this discussion, to visualise the range of possibilities open. The form's contribution might be in terms of, e.g., making some arrangements (publicity, food, etc.), organising a party game, or providing a short item of entertainment.

Use the discussion to further skills in frameworks and agendas. Work through small groups.

The framework for the meeting will need to have been thought out in advance, e.g. as a guide to the number of young people being prepared to make statements.

The responsibility for reporting back is very important.

STAGE 9

Autumn Term

PROGRAMME

Greetings and caring.

Report the second year meeting:
1 The second year Christmas event:
  (a) Report from the representatives of the group who attended the meeting:

  (i) The general decision of the meeting.
  (ii) The way the group's own proposals were received.
  (iii) A clear statement about the part to be played by this group.
  (b) Small group discussion and open decisions about how the group's obligations are to be met.

2 The 'How do we find school?' enquiry:
  (a) An account of the main matters raised at the year meeting.
  (b) How the group's own submissions were received.
  (c) The main outcome of the meeting.
  (d) Is anything required of this group?

Caring and friendship:
  'What kind of friend am I?' – using **Working Paper 18** as an agenda for small group discussions with some open exchanges.

OBJECTIVES AND COMMENTS

This has a threefold purpose:
  (a) to prepare for the Christmas event;
  (b) to extend the discussion about progress in school;
  (c) to practise agendas, frameworks and public statements. This will be reinforced at Stages 15 and 16.

The Christmas event – what is the group's contribution to be? Get clear decisions and assignment of roles.

Progress in school – focus on responsibilities of the group. Some response from the senior staff will need to be *seen* to have taken place for the exercise to carry credibility.

Revive the discussion of friendship to lead into a series on peer relationships in Stages 10 to 12.

STAGE 10

PROGRAMME

Greetings and caring.

Personal responsibilities in befriending others:
Through small group discussion and open exchanges.

(a) How important to us are our friends?

(b) Have you ever felt lonely?

(c) Are there lonely people around us, or people who feel short of friends?

(d) Is there anything we could do to befriend those people?

Role-play as appropriate.

Second year Christmas event:
Are we clear about the arrangements, and about the contribution to be made by individual small groups and people?

Progress with school work – fourth self-assessment using **Working Paper 29**. Give some serious consideration to personal objectives arising out of the self-assessment.

Reporting school experience to parents – working through small group discussion and open exchanges. What should we be reporting to our parents, and discussing with them

(a) about the people we meet at school and how we get on with them?

(b) the group activities we take part in?

(c) our progress with lessons and homework?

Should we share our self-assessment with them, and the objectives we have suggested for ourselves? How will you approach this? Role-play your approach.

OBJECTIVES AND COMMENTS

Encourage members of the group to consider and extend their own ability to help other people. There may be some immediate needs in their own group. But this depends upon the people concerned being able to accept their advances. Some close personal and introspective discussion may arise.

Organisational responsibilities need to be clearly accepted, together with the support required to help the young people to see them through.

This self-assessment is about getting on top of this year's work. Thinking forward to third year subject choices can probably wait until Stage 22 in the Spring term. A copy of **Working Paper 29** will be required for each pupil. The tutor will need to see the completed papers.

Members of the group could help one another in small groups to complete the self-assessment and state their objectives, which will be looked at more closely in Stage 11.

In the hope that the pupils can engage their parents in a continuing conversation about their school work.

Leads to an occasion for parents in the Summer term (Stages 33 to 35), but earlier consultation with the form teacher might be appropriate for some. This will need to be considered when briefing the group members for their reporting to their parents.

STAGE 11

PROGRAMME

Greetings and caring.

Christmas event:
  Rehearse the group's contribution.

Consolidate trust and caring between girls and boys:
  Trust walk with mixed partners as far as posssible.

Ease of conversations between girls and boys – agendas:
  In mixed small groups of, say, four young people, work through the agenda in **Working Paper 19**, followed by short public statements.

Report conversations with parents:
  Compare experience in small groups, and prepare for brief open exchanges. Is there anything we should be doing as a whole group?

Progress at school:
  Small groups and some open exchanges.

  (a) Review the objectives arising from the fourth self-assessment.
  (b) Plan any consultation with teachers that is required.
  (c) Consider strategies for moving towards personal objectives.

OBJECTIVES AND COMMENTS

The Christmas event will take place before the next stage.

An attempt to ease the contact between girls and boys, and to deepen their understanding of what it is like to be in the other's shoes.

The second part of **Working Paper 19** will reinforce the skill in constructing agendas and frameworks, and in making public statements.

The experience will also prepare for any mixed activities that are to be part of the Christmas event. You may wish to have a copy of the working paper for each small group.

The form tutor may be able to judge from the exchanges whether formal contact with parents can be left until Stage 22 in the Spring term (on the basis of the fifth self-assessment, **Working Paper 30**), or whether some prior action will be required. Here is an opportunity to check whether any parents should be invited to the school.

The personal objectives and strategies should be written out, so that they can be revived at the beginning of next term.

STAGE 12   *Autumn Term*

(Final stage before Christmas break.)

PROGRAMME

Greetings.

Caring and administration:
  Review methods and this term's experience. Plan for next term.

Assemblies:
  Consider the possibility of the group taking responsibility for one of the year assemblies next term. Small groups – brainstorming – some ideas about the form the assembly could take.

The Christmas event – some stocktaking. General views about the event – what would we do next year if we were to have another event? Critical appraisal of the group's contribution.

Girls and boys:
  Small groups and open exchanges. Are some people embarrassed when they have to meet, work with, or converse with a boy or girl? Why are they embarrassed? Is it easier for us now? Do we treat a boy or girl with the same courtesy as we would a fellow girl or boy? Should we treat him or her with any special courtesy or consideration?

Adieus and good wishes for the Christmas holidays:
  Will you be doing anything special? Are there any arrangements to meet?

OBJECTIVES AND COMMENTS

Serious stocktaking. Complete the revision of approach in Stage 13 next term.

Only discuss tentative plans at this stage – and get used to the idea. Make firm plans in the first stage of next term.

An opportunity to note ideas for next year. Some self-criticism might be appropriate.

Should lead to some discussion of the normative controls that often inhibit boys and girls from meeting and behaving easily with one another.

Leave enough time for hand-taking and general good wishes – with a reminder about meeting the boys (or girls) also.

PLANNING SCHEDULE: YEAR TWO

THEME	STAGE 13	STAGE 14	STAGE 15	STAGE 16	STAGE 17	STAGE 18
The pupil's place in the school	Plan contribution to assembly.*	Rehearse contribution to assembly.**		Statements about school (agendas/frameworks). *	**	Ideas for assembly.**
Caring community	Revise caring/administration. Consider group programme for term.*					Review of caring/administration.*
Relationships, the self and social skills					Roles in life.*	Gender roles**
Communications skills				Communication workshop. public statements. ***	**	
School work and study skills	Revise personal objectives.**	Note taking.***	Note taking (visitor).**	Compare notes. Review progress towards objectives.**		
Academic guidance and careers education						
Health and hygiene	Keeping healthy.*	Keeping healthy—preparation for a visitor.*	Keeping healthy—a visitor.***			
Personal interests						

STAGE 13   *Spring Term*

(First stage after Christmas break.)

PROGRAMME

Greetings:
How did you find the Christmas holidays?

Caring:
Who is absent and what do we know about them?
Revise arrangements for caring and admin-
istration.

Settle plans for a year assembly:
Allocate roles and responsibilities.

Group programme:
Look forward to the main items in this term's
programme. Are there any other items that
should be included? (Small working parties and
open exchanges.)

Progress in school:
Revise the objectives agreed last term. Determine
action to be taken – work in small support
groups.

Keeping healthy:
Small groups and open exchanges. Coping with
the winter months – do we need to give some
things special attention? (a) Hygiene and
cleanliness? (b) Exercise? (c) Food? (d) Weight
watching? (e) Sleep? (f) Smoking? Look forward
to receiving a visitor in Stage 15.

OBJECTIVES AND COMMENTS

Meeting and greeting. Rebuild the momentum.
Encourage girls and boys to greet following on
last term.

Some changes in method may be required. Change
who does what to extend the experience. Could
offer some important experience to those who
need it.

Assuming that there is time, a rehearsal of the
assembly can be left to Stage 14.

The main items in the planning schedule for the first
half of the term would form the basic
information. It is important that the group
should be identified with the programme. A small
working party might be formed to look through
the programme with the tutor.

Consider the formation of longer-term small groups
to support one another in coping with school
work, including homework – academic support
groups.

To loosen up discussion in readiness to receive a
specialist in health education as a visitor in Stage
15. Detailed preparation can be left to Stage 14.

STAGE 14   *Spring Term*

PROGRAMME

Greetings and caring:
   Are the new arrangements made for caring and
   administration working properly?

Year assembly:
   Rehearse the group's conduct of a year assembly.

Keeping healthy:
   What are the questions we wish to raise with the
   visitor,
   (a) in order to know the visitor personally?
   (b) about health – building on the discussions in
       Stage 13?
   Who will make the introductions and conclude?
   (Role-play this.)

Note taking:
   Reversing the process learnt in building frameworks and agendas to form the basis of statements and conversations. What are the key ideas
   being expressed in oral statements? How briefly
   can we express those ideas in note form?
   Work in small groups who will listen to several
   accounts from members of the group about, e.g.,
   Christmas day; coming to school this morning;
   what I did last night; my attempts to keep fit.
   Each small group will decide what were the basic
   ideas, and note them. Compare the notes of one
   group with others. Look forward to making notes
   about what the visitor says in Stage 15.

OBJECTIVES AND COMMENTS

The framework and individual contributions
   should be settled and rehearsed at this stage. If
   the group's assembly is to come later in the term,
   a brief revision and rehearsal may be needed
   immediately before the date.

Although the visitor will be chosen as someone who
   can inform the group about keeping healthy, the
   conversation should begin by getting to know
   about the visitor as a person. Throughout the
   young people should be initiating the dialogue.

The practice in agendas and frameworks should
   have been a useful preparation for dealing with
   note taking. The emphasis of this exercise is on
   noting oral statements.

The tutor may have to begin the statements and
   should have something already thought out. Try
   several rapid exercises. Several young people
   could have been briefed beforehand to have a
   description ready.

The purpose at this stage is to get over the principle
   of seizing the basic ideas being expressed.

STAGE 15

PROGRAMME

Greetings and caring.

Note taking:
Organise through small groups, possibly each noting only part of the proceedings. More than one group should note each section of the conversation so that they can compare their notes with one another. The groups to check the notes they have taken. Reports from the small groups to the whole group can be extended into Stage 16.

Keeping healthy – a visitor:
(a) Prepare for note taking.
(b) Revise agenda.
(c) Revise arrangements for reception and conclusion and role-play if necessary.

Receive the visitor.

(a) What did we learn?
(b) How well did we cope?

OBJECTIVES AND COMMENTS

Keep in mind the several objectives.

(a) Constructing frameworks and agendas.
(b) Initiating the visit with a personal conversation.
(c) Young people should retain responsibility for initiating the conversation about keeping healthy, but the visitor should be free to develop points not raised by the young people.
(d) The group should encourage those members to take part for whom it would be an appropriate next step.
(e) Note taking to be an important by-product of the visit. (The visitor should be informed that this is taking place.) The comparison of notes can be extended into Stage 16.

STAGE 16

Spring Term

PROGRAMME

Greetings and caring.

Note taking:
Comparing notes taken during the visit – each group to report their notes for comparison and comment.

Progress in school:
The small academic support groups to review each individual's objectives and the progress made towards those objectives. (Refer to **Working Paper 29**, Stages 10 and 11.) A brief exchange of information between the groups.

Communications workshop:
A concentration on non-verbal communication in a step-by-step programme following **Working Paper 24**. To be continued in Stage 17.

Speaking to the whole group – public statements:
Small groups to prepare, rehearse and deliver statements lasting, say, two or three minutes, to the whole group. For subject matter, revert to the discussion about school in Stages 7 to 9. Suggest a number of titles,
e.g. My ideal school.
Is school really necessary?
School and life.
To be continued in Stage 17.

OBJECTIVES AND COMMENTS

Are the *basic ideas* being caught?
(a) Notes as an *aide-memoire* for the person writing them.
(b) *Economy* of words as basic to note taking.

Encourage skill in mutual long-term support, which can continue when teachers are not available. Some emphasis on cooperation rather than competition within the group may be appropriate.

The exploration of non-verbal communication may touch some young people very deeply. It is much more than the practice of a few skills – it may enter and allow expression of deeper feelings, including feelings about self. The tutor may be able to engage some group members in an important extension of the means of expression and of social skills.

This is to reinforce the skills of constructing frameworks and agendas, cooperative planning, making statements in public.

It is important that the small groups take responsibility for helping one another – the bold member to give way and to encourage the more timid member. Some of the statements could be a symposium, involving all the members of the group. A number of the groups will readily suggest their own titles.

STAGE 17

PROGRAMME

Greetings and caring.

Continuing the communication workshop:
Continue with **Working Paper 24**. Use some kind of warm-up before beginning on later exercises.

Speaking to the whole group:
(a) Encourage the groups that have not yet presented their statements to revise their preparation.
(b) Encourage the other groups to offer critical support following each statement. Very brief small group discussions at the end of each statement could prepare for this.

The roles we play – a number of roles in life. Socratic discussion – interspersed with role-play, exploring the variety of roles that members of the group are required to play at home, at school, with friends and with playmates. Use Section one of **Working Paper 23**. How far are these roles imposed upon us, and how far do we create them?

OBJECTIVES AND COMMENTS

As the exploration goes deeper, so the individual positions of each group member should be borne in mind, so that individuals can be offered opportunities for appropriate personal experience. Encourage the small groups to have this in mind.

There should be a growth in assurance as the experience of the whole group increases. Encourage the small groups to be concerned also with the development of their members who find public statements difficult. Lead the support. Make sure that comments take into account the kind of effort required of a timid or inarticulate member of the group.

Although a number of roles are prescribed by the customs of our society, each individual is playing his/her roles in his/her own individual way – even by conformity!

The purpose of the exercise is to come to understand the concept of roles, and the creative part that each one can play in their formation.

Leave gender roles to be dealt with in Stage 18.

STAGE 18   *Spring Term*

(*Last stage before half-term break.*)

PROGRAMME

Greetings.

Caring:
Review the approach to caring and administration in readiness for next half term.

Second year assembly:
Working parties to produce ideas for an assembly
next term. Preliminary allocation of responsibilities – to follow up possibilities.

The roles we play:
Complete *Section One* of **Working Paper 23**.
Concentrate on gender roles, following *Section
Two* of **Working Paper 23**. Work towards an
increasing sensitivity and understanding in be-
haviour between boys and girls.

Half-term break:
Have you any special plans? Arrangements for
any sub-group activities. Adieus and good
wishes.

OBJECTIVES AND COMMENTS

How well is this going? Review carefully the
administration that you are dealing with, and see
whether anything more can be shared with the
group members.

It may be possible for one or two members of the
group to do the necessary research or enquiry
about suitable material during the Easter
holidays.

The discussion should be moving steadily towards
an examination of the individual's own style of
behaviour. Some young people may need strong
support from the group as they question their
own behaviour. This will be picked up again in
Stage 19. The discussion about gender roles
should also initiate the increasing attention that
will be given in later programmes to responsible
behaviour between boys and girls, young men
and young women.

PLANNING SCHEDULE: YEAR TWO

THEME	STAGE 19	STAGE 20	STAGE 21	STAGE 22	STAGE 23	STAGE 24
The pupil's place in the school		Rehearsal for assembly.*	Review of group's behaviour.**	Review of group's behaviour.**	Review of group's behaviour—progress report.*	Ideas for next assembly.*
Caring community	Recommence caring/administration. Renew support.*					Review of caring. Farewells and arrangements for Easter holidays.*
Relationships, the self and social skills	The way we play our roles.**	Resilience to criticism. Fear of rejection.**	Coping with conflict.**	Progress report and further action.**	Progress report.*	
Communication skills						
School work and study skills			Comparing notes.**	Fifth self-assessment.**	Declaration of objectives. Sharing with parents.**	Personal strategies. *
Academic guidance and careers education						
Health and hygine	Our developing bodies—preparation for a visitor.***	Our developing bodies—a visitor.***				
Personal interests	Knowing our own district—a visitor.***				Knowing our own district.**	Knowing our own district—a visitor.***

STAGE 19   *Spring Term*

(*First stage after half-term break.*)

PROGRAMME

Greetings:
An emphasis on renewing support and contracts – some very personal sessions are to follow.

Caring and administration:
Set in motion the arrangements agreed in Stage 18.

The way we play our roles:
Small group discussion and open exchanges.

(a) Do I behave in many ways that are sometimes not helpful to me and to other people? Show me (use role-play) to make sure that I can see it from your viewpoint.
(b) Are other people influencing me to behave in this way?
(c) What kind of changes might I consider?
(d) Are there things that we could all do to help?

Our developing bodies:
Preparation for an incisive conversation with a specialist visitor. Small group discussions (probably small groups of boys or girls only) and open exchanges. How much have you grown during the last year? How much taller are you? Do you know your weight? Has it made any difference to the way you use your arms and legs? Has your face changed? Have you noticed any other changes like being hungry or sleepy? How are you finding the sexual developments that are taking place, e.g. menstruation, development of breasts in the girls, growth of pubic hair, the emission of semen in the boys, and the increase in sexual feeling? Is there anything that you do not understand or would like to know more about? Is there anything that you are anxious about?

Preparation for the visitor:
(a) Meeting and greeting the visitor. Who will take responsibility for introducing and concluding? (For whom would this be useful experience?)

OBJECTIVES AND COMMENTS

Mutual support will be vital to the programme for the rest of this term. If necessary, repeat a support exercise, e.g. trust walk or rocking.

An opportunity to build on the insights gained in Stages 17 and 18. Special attention to role behaviours that are unhelpful to individual young people and their peers.
Explore through role-play. Focus on any group reinforcement of roles. Help individuals to set personal objectives and strategies. Engage the group in supporting their movement – in some cases the support of the whole group may be required.

A good deal of knowledge will have reached the young people about their physical development, including through lessons in school.

The purpose here is more to find out whether there are gaps in their knowledge, and to explore any anxieties they may have about their physical development. Some feelings about body image may be important here.

There is a danger that the later attention to sexual development may swamp the earlier discussion, so notes should be made about the earlier matters raised as the discussion proceeds. Some important anxieties about body image may be beneath some of the earlier discussions.

Formal note taking about the matters raised will ensure that delicate issues are not pushed aside later.

The choice of persons to receive and thank the visitor may have relevance to the earlier discussion about roles and role modification. (The same applies to the allocation of roles for the assembly.)

PROGRAMME

  (b) Getting to know the visitor as a person –
      agenda.

  (c) Raising our questions – what questions? –
      and who will initiate each part of the
      discussion?

  (d) Should we invite the visitor to add anything
      else that might be helpful? Who will do this?

Revise ideas for assembly. Allocate roles. Rehearsal
in Stage 20.

OBJECTIVES AND COMMENTS

It is important that individual members of the
group make a firm undertaking to raise specific
questions – and some rehearsal may be required
to ensure that they feel adequate in doing so.

STAGE 20   *Spring Term*

PROGRAMME

Greetings and support in readiness for the visitor.

Caring and administration.

Rehearsal for year assembly.

Our developing bodies:
Revise preparation for the visitor.

(a) Role-play reception and conclusion.
(b) Rehearse a number of the questions.
(c) Arrange for note taking – sharing responsibility around.

Receive the visitor.

(a) Review what were the more important issues raised.
(b) How well did we cope?
(c) A more detailed comparison of notes in Stage 21.

Coping with people:
Small group discussion with open exchanges.

(a) When people criticise me I . . .
(b) When someone is unkind to me I . . .
(c) If there is a danger of my being left out, or I feel I am not wanted, I . . .

Explore some of the statements through role-play.

OBJECTIVES AND COMMENTS

Reinforce support in coping with emotionally charged discussion.

See that individual young people are secure in their roles and are able to cope with any emotionally charged questions.

Follow up of note taking exercises.

An immediate exchange in order to consolidate a dialogue about delicate subjects and possibly using a new vocabulary.

This is about developing a resilience to criticism and unkindness, and coping with a fear of rejection. Their own fears often cause people to read into a situation more than is really there. In a single session you may be able to do little more than help young people to be conscious of their reactions, so that they may begin to cope with their own feelings. They may be able to help one another in this. This theme is continued in Stage 21.

STAGE 21   *Spring Term*

| PROGRAMME | OBJECTIVES AND COMMENTS |

PROGRAMME

Greeting and caring.

Review of the group's behaviour:
  Small group discussion and open exchanges.
  How do we see our group's behaviour in the
  school?
    What are our strengths?
    What are our weaknesses?

What do we mean by *responsible* behaviour?
  Is it only doing what we are told?
  Does it involve any positive action on our part?

How do other people see us? Prepare for action
research.
  Small groups to meet and question:
  (a) year head,
  (b) several teachers that the class meets often;
  (c) a number of parents.

Formulate brief enquiry, e.g.

  (a) What do you see as the strong points of our
      form?
  (b) What do you see as our weak points?
  (c) What would you most like us to give attention
      to?
  (d) We are discussing what we mean by *re-
      sponsible* behaviour – in what ways is this
      different from doing what we are told?
Contracts to see the enquiry through and report
back in Stage 22.

Our developing bodies – comparing notes: Hear
from each small group about the notes that they
have made. Stimulate discussion about some of
the main issues raised.

Coping with people – coping with conflict:
  In small groups, discuss:
  (a) When someone is rude to me I . . .
  (b) When someone threatens me I . . .
  (c) When a teacher reprimands me I . . .
  (d) When my parents are cross with me I . . .
  (e) When one of my friends gets angry with me
      I . . .

OBJECTIVES AND COMMENTS

The focus is on *responsible* rather than conformist
behaviour. Responsible may imply some initiative when there is no one at hand to direct the
young people.

Action research, so that the young people will make
their own discoveries, and, it is hoped, will be
moved by those discoveries to take appropriate
action. Each small group to be responsible for
approaching one or two people only.

Keep the enquiry simple and brief. Role-play
conducting the enquiry, and illustrate how a
conversation can arise, rather than a question
and answer exchange.

Firm contracts required. The small groups may be
responsible for the joint action of their members.

Consolidate the discussion, acclimatise the young
people to handling the terms used, and establish
the topics as a normal part of the group's interest
and discussion.

Warm to the topic through small group discussion.
Then explore the behaviour through role-play.

Get the young people to consider alternative strategies and role-play these.

PROGRAMME

Strategies for coping:
Role-play in the full group one of the statements made. Now try a different response – not by giving way, but by being calm and reasonable. What could this be? Try it in role-play. Now role-play something similar in small groups.

Discussion in small groups.
(a) When I am faced by . . . I should like to be able to . . .
(b) Contracts for individual action and small group support.

OBJECTIVES AND COMMENTS

Engage the small groups in supporting one another in a determination to try out new strategies and report back experience.

STAGE 22

Spring Term

PROGRAMME

Greetings and caring.

Review of the group's behaviour:
Report from small groups.
1 The group's behaviour:
  (a) What were said to be the group's strong points?
  (b) What were the weak points?
  (c) What was it suggested we should give most attention to?
  (d) What do we think?

2 Responsible behaviour:
  (a) What was suggested to us was the meaning of responsible behaviour?
  (b) What do we think?

3 Decision and action:
  (a) Decide ways in which we wish to modify our behaviour as a group.
  (b) Decide ways in which we can extend the range of our responsible behaviour.
  (c) Agree the first steps. Report progress in Stage 23.
  (d) Form small groups to record decisions and intention.

Coping with people – criticism, rejection, conflict:
  (a) Report individual progress in small groups.
  (b) Exchange information in the whole group.
  (c) Role-play some of the scenes described.
  (d) Review coping strategies and renew contracts for individual action and small group support.

Progress with school work – self-assessment:
  (a) Review the academic support groups.
  (b) Complete *Part I* of **Working Paper 30** individually. Discuss your answers with your small group.
  (c) Use *Part II* of **Working Paper 30** as an agenda for discussion in your small group so that you can help one another consider your own study skills. Look at one question at a time; discuss it, and then write your own answer.

OBJECTIVES AND COMMENTS

Small groups to prepare statements about what they have discovered. (Revive agendas/frameworks and public statements. Small groups to support their spokesman – and should choose members for whom this would be a valuable experience).

Discoveries should lead straight to action. Strategies and objectives will need to be realistic, and probably quite limited.

Discussion of responsible behaviour could lead to limited, but quite important initiatives. What would be helpful in school or to other people around them?

Progress report, redefining objectives, and decisions about action.

A copy of **Working Paper 30** will be required for each pupil.

Focus on the value of the small groups supporting their members in schoolwork.

It may be profitable to place some emphasis at this stage on Part II, some general study skills. If a pupil suggests some that are not listed, see that this is brought out in the open, as there are likely to be others affected in the same way.

PROGRAMME

(d) Complete Part III. You will not be able to manage too much at once, so think carefully about priorities.

OBJECTIVES AND COMMENTS

The papers, when collected, will need some analysis to see where most urgent action is required. Could your caring/administration team help you here?

STAGE 23

Spring Term

PROGRAMME

Greetings and caring.

Group's behaviour:
Back to small groups. Review the past weeks efforts and events. How far are we being success-ful in moving towards our objectives? Are our objectives realistic? Review them and make a renewed decision for action.

Coping with people:
Back to small support groups. Restatement of personal objectives and an account of recent experience. Review objectives and contracts for continued action.

Progress in school:
Review of fifth self-assessment **Working Paper 30** in the small support groups. Review of the summary and objectives of each person. Plan strategies, including consultation with subject teachers. Consider what needs to be done by or on behalf of the group as a whole. What contri-bution will be required of the group tutor?

How will we share the progress report and intended strategies with our parents? Small group dis-cussion to settle approaches to be adopted. What are your parents' views of your progress?

Knowing our own district:
Working through small groups, what do you know about –

(a) Buildings – when they were built, by whom, and in what style?
(b) Industries and occupations? and what hap-pens in the local commercial centres?
(c) Where people live, the kinds of accommo-dation available, and when the estates were developed?

OBJECTIVES AND COMMENTS

Keep interests and determination alive. The tutor will be contributing his own observations about the group's recent efforts and behaviour.

Maintain an emphasis on *responsible* behaviour. What initiatives are open to the group?

This is as far as the topic can be taken at this stage. But now that the matter has been raised to a conscious level, there will be many opportunities to build on good intentions.

For some, progress must be about individual effort, but in other cases, subject teachers must be involved. Help the young people to plan their consultation with other members of staff – in so far as they are capable of taking this on. You may need to ease the way in some cases.

There may be some fairly urgent matters that go beyond subject responsibilities, in which case wider staff consultation and decision may be required.

Are you reaching a stage where the parent could be encouraged to report the pupil's progress from his viewpoint?

An attempt to enrich young people's normal daily contacts with the home district, and to engage their interest in local affairs.

Some tentative enquiries to be conducted by the small groups.

Continued overleaf

PROGRAMME

(d) Public entertainment, clubs, restaurants? Recreation and sports facilities? Museums?

(e) Do you know the history of the town – or even why it is here?

Your group should decide what to be interested in. Consult parents and anyone else you think can help you.

Prepare for a visitor in Stage 24.

OBJECTIVES AND COMMENTS

Preparation for the visitor in Stage 24 can arise out of this experience. The visitor will have been chosen on account of his local knowledge.

STAGE 24   *Spring Term*

(Final stage before Easter break.)

PROGRAMME

OBJECTIVES AND COMMENTS

Greetings.

Review of caring and administration in readiness
for next term.

Progress in school:
(a) Report of individual action – first to small   If longer term consultation and help is required, this
    support groups, followed by some open   will need to be kept alive into next term.
    exchanges.
(b) Report of consultation and contacts with
    subject teachers.
(c) Report of conversations with parents. Is there
    any way in which they could share our self-
    assessment and reporting next time?

Knowing our own district:
Small group discussion and open reports. What   The purpose here is not so much to inform the
have you learnt about your district? Preparation   young people about their district, as to
for specialist visitor:
(a) Agenda for a personal conversation.   (a) engage their continuing interest;
(b) What questions do we want to raise about   (b) to help them understand how to enquire and
    our locality – who will initiate the questions?   what there is to enquire about. (In any case,
(c) Who will receive and introduce the visitor   not all the pupils necessarily come from the
    and who will conclude?   same district.)

Receive the visitor.

Follow-up of visit. Let us see what we can   A very minor project is suggested for the Easter
discover during the Easter holdiday. Each small   holidays, although some of the young people may
group will take on a limited piece of enquiry, and be interested enough to spend some time at it.
report back in Stage 25.   This is the beginning of a more outward-looking
                                                    programme with increasing interest in the sur-
                                                    rounding community (picked up again in Stages
                                                    27–30).

PLANNING SCHEDULE: YEAR TWO

THEME	STAGE 25	STAGE 26	STAGE 27	STAGE 28	STAGE 29	STAGE 30
The pupil's place in the school	Plan assembly.*	Rehearse assembly.*				
Caring community	Revise caring. Group's programme for this term.**					
Relationships, the self and social skills	Cooperation with teachers and school. Planning empathy.***	Role-play and role-reversal.***	Consultation. Teacher as a visitor.***			
Communication skills			Our community—other people's lives and interests. Prepare for action research.**	Begin action research.**	Conclude action research—report.**	Visitors (leading to responsibility and authority).***
School work and study skills		Being inventive and imaginative.**				
Academic guidance and careers education						
Health and hygiene						
Personal interests	Know our district. Personal investigation during Easter holiday.*			(a) Personal statements. (b) Prepare for a visitor.***	Our interests and enthusiasms. Visitor.***	Activities I would like to take up.**

STAGE 25

(*First stage after Easter break.*)

PROGRAMME

Greetings:
Renew contracts for Summer term.

Caring and administration:
Set in motion the plans made at the end of last term.

Group programme:
Look at plans for the term.

Assembly:
Plan for a second year assembly this term.

Knowing our own district:
A report from the small groups about observation during the Easter holidays.

Empathy exercise – putting ourselves in other people's shoes:
(a) Shadowing.
(b) Personal conversations in twos guided by a series of questions posed by the tutor. Reports and introductions in the first person in fours. A guide to this empathy exercise will be found in **Working Paper 25**.

OBJECTIVES AND COMMENTS

A special effort is required:
(a) to renew support and contracts within the group;
(b) to reinforce self-help in the group through the caring and administration programme;
(c) to gain the young people's identification with the group's programme, through consultation about the term's work.

A further opportunity for individuals to make statements to the whole group. The small group should encourage some who have not yet done this to report on their behalf.

The empathy exercise is intended as a lead into the next phase of work, and to prepare the young people to put themselves into the shoes first, of their teachers (Stages 26–27), and second, of other people in the surrounding community (Stages 27–30).

STAGE 26

PROGRAMME

Greetings and caring.

Rehearse the group's second year assembly.

Our teachers – what is it like to be a teacher in this school? Preparation for a conversation with a teacher as visitor in Stage 27.

  (a) Role-play and role-reversal – role-play scenes, e.g.

  – encouraging pupils to feel that they can succeed;
  – coping with cheeky members of the class;
  – sorting out a quarrel at the back of the class;
  – about an imagined conversation between the teacher and colleagues in the staffroom after a difficult lesson;
  – about a teacher hearing from year head/ head of school about a complaint from a parent.

  (b) Small groups consider some of the things they would like to say to teachers about the school.

  (c) Small group discussions and open exchanges. What do you think it is like to be a teacher in this school?

  (d) Small groups to consider questions about being a teacher that could be raised with a teacher as visitor to the group in Stage 27.

Spontaneity workshop:
  – being inventive and imaginative. Use familiar aspects of life in a novel and fantastic way. A framework is provided by **Working Paper 26**, but before long the members of the group should be able to suggest (invent) their own prompts.

OBJECTIVES AND COMMENTS

This represents an application of the skills of empathy to the position of the teacher, and is intended to give young people a greater contact with the teacher and insights into the teacher's work.

A teacher will be required as a visitor in Stage 27. It may be necessary to exchange tutors between groups in order to make teachers available.

This should be conducted at a fairly brisk pace – rather like brainstorming. Spontaneity is related to empathy, and quick inventiveness will support the formulation of frameworks and agendas, and many other aspects of school work.

Once this style of work has been established, it would be possible to fit supplementary work in even the odd ten minutes.

STAGE 27

PROGRAMME

Greetings and caring.

Relationships with teachers:
 Receive a teacher as a visitor.
 (a) Revise agenda:
  holding a personal conversation, showing an interest in his/her being a teacher.
 (b) Role-play reception and conclusion.

 Meet the visitor-teacher:
 (a) How well did we cope?
 (b) What did we learn?
 (c) How are we involved as pupils in all this?
 (d) Is there any long-term action required of us?

Other people in our local community – their lives and their interests:
 Could we come to understand more of what goes on around us (empathy with other people in the community)? We shall want to know about their work and how they spend their day, about their family responsibilities and about their interests. We will all contract to interview two or three people whom we can contact easily. So let us consider in small groups, with open reports:

 (a) the kinds of people that each one of us could meet easily;
 (b) the kinds of things that we should be interested in (broad headings);
 (c) the prompts within those headings.

No other action is needed until Stage 28 – just turn the topic over in the mind.

OBJECTIVES AND COMMENTS

Merely to deepen the understanding between pupil and teacher may be all that is required.

But it is possible that some kind of modification of behaviour is called for. The young people can take this into their long-term action. If this cannot be accomplished by the young people alone, it may be necessary to establish a dialogue with a certain teacher or teachers, so that a satisfactory working arrangement between pupils and teacher can be effected.

This represents a natural progression from an interest in *things* in our neighbourhood last term to people this term. It also follows up empathy and relationships with teachers – and now relationships with other adults.

It is suggested that young people should meet adults in their neighbourhood through action research, and that they should share their discoveries with a visitor – someone with a lively interest in community affairs. An example of the kind of enquiry that would be appropriate is given in **Working Paper 22**.

You may wish to have a small working party of young people to help finalise the enquiry sheet.

STAGE 28

PROGRAMME

Greetings and caring.

Relationships with teachers:
  Is there any action to report?

Other people in our community:
  (a) Review the form of enquiry.
  (b) In small groups settle the people whom each member will contact. Open report.
  (c) Role-play the approach to the conversation, first as an open demonstration, and then in small groups. Each member of the group to rehearse his or her approach.
  (d) Make clear contracts that each will carry through his conversations.

Our interests and enthusiasms:
  (a) What are your interests? Discussion in small groups.
  (b) One minute statements from individual members of the group – statements to be rehearsed in small groups.
  (c) Prepare to receive a visitor who is knowledgable about interests and activities. Small groups will suggest items for the agenda for a conversation with the visitor,
     (i) personal interest in the visitor,
     (ii) conversation about his own interests,
     (iii) and about interests and activities suitable for young people.

OBJECTIVES AND COMMENTS

The form of enquiry will have been finalised in association with a small working party from the group. Sufficient copies should be available for each member of the group to conduct at least two conversations. An example of the kinds of headings and prompts that may be suitable are given in **Working Paper 22**. Meeting other adults will be a significant experience for the young people, and some of them will need considerable rehearsal and support if they are to carry it through. The less confident may wish to tackle this together with another member of the group. Take the contracts quite seriously. The tutor should follow this up and reinforce their determination on any occasion that he meets the group. The exercise is leading to a report back in Stage 29 and consultation with a visitor in Stage 30.

This discussion is intended to encourage the interests and hobbies of the young people, and specifically to look forward to the light summer evenings and holidays. Any relevance to the half-term break could be especially helpful. A visitor is required for Stage 29, with lively personal interests and fairly wide knowledge of other interests.

STAGE 29   *Summer Term*

PROGRAMME

Greetings and caring.

Other people in our community:
  (a) Progress report in small groups.
  (b) Small group reports to whole group.
  (c) Role-play some experiences, both successful and difficult.
  (d) Make plans for an extension of the enquiry. Contracts in small groups and open exchanges.
  (e) Draw up agenda for discussion with visitor in Stage 29. Small group discussion and open exchanges.

Our interests and enthusiasms – meeting a visitor:
  (a) Revise the agenda.
  (b) Allocate responsibilities for introductions, initiation of discussion and conclusions.
  (c) Role-play.

Meet the visitor.
  (a) Review:
      What did we learn?
      How well did we cope?
  (b) Preparation in small groups for Stage 30, with personal statements:
      – the activities I would like to take up;
      – the steps I might take.

Ideas for a parents' evenings towards the end of the summer term:
Small group discussion and open exchanges.

  (a) What do we want to share with our parents, – about school or in general?
  (b) What form could a parents' evening take?
  (c) Fix the date and consider the way that parents should be invited to attend.

OBJECTIVES AND COMMENTS

Make sure that the whole group learns about the successes, but at the same time offers strong support to those who are finding it difficult to approach outside adults. Some careful planning and preparation may be required to enable some young people to dare to make the approach. Joint approaches shared with a more confident colleague may be required, but still involving the less confident in their share of the conversation.

You have the half-term and the summer holidays in mind as well as a long term development of interests.

If your visitor is concerned with recreational facilities or an evening centre, the young people may be able to make immediate arrangements to meet him there.

You will be returning to personal interests related to the summer holidays in Stages 35 and 36.

The introduction of the idea of an evening with the parents of this form. A short brainstorming session to throw up suggestions about the purpose of the event and the possible forms it could take, to initiate some general thinking – more detailed discussion in Stage 31. Some ideas for a parents' evening are given in **Working Paper 17**.

STAGE 30   *Summer Term*

(*Last stage before half-term break.*)

PROGRAMME

Greetings and caring.

Other people in our community:
  (a) Report action research in small groups with open exchanges.
  (b) Revise agenda for visitor:
      – interest in the visitor as a person;
      – other people in the community.
  (c) Preparation for reception and conclusion. Meet the visitor.

  (a) Review what has been exchanged.
  (b) How well did we cope?
  (c) Look forward to 'authority in the community'.

Interests and enthusiasms:
  Statements to the whole group about 'activities that I would like to take up'.

  (a) Preparation in small groups – the activity, what I would hope to get out of it, how I might go about it.
  (b) Personal statements to the whole group.
  (c) Response from the group with questions and suggestions.

Ideas for assembly next half-term.

OBJECTIVES AND COMMENTS

One of the effects of action research is that the participants' discoveries will stir them into action. You will be hoping that the experience will lead quite naturally into a discussion about the exercise of authority in the community in Stages 31 and 32 (and you need to brief your visitor carefully in this respect). The outcome is likely to be quite modest, such as a growth in a sense of responsibility on the part of young people within their community. This might take a specific form, such as the discouragement of vandalism, or an increase of care of the environment – tidiness and less litter.

You will be using this also to develop skills in public statements, but on this occasion try to arrange a follow-up dialogue between the speaker and audience through questions and suggestions. You may need a few moments small-group discussion from time to time to stimulate this.

A brief brainstorming session. Notes should be taken to help immediate decisions in Stage 31.

PLANNING SCHEDULE: YEAR TWO

THEME	STAGE 31	STAGE 32	STAGE 33	STAGE 34	STAGE 35	STAGE 36
The pupil's place in the school	Assembly—decisions and rehearsal.**	Planning parents' evening.*	Planning parents' evening.*	Planning parents' evening.*	Parents' evening.*	
Caring community	Responsibility and authority in the community.					
Relationships, the self and social skills	Prepare for a visitor.**	Visitor.**	Prepare enquiry with parents.***	Action research with parents—report.**	Review of parents' evening.**	Family—the part that we can play.**
Communication skills	Exploratory discussion (parents' evening).**	Formal meetings (to decide about parents. evening).*		Coping with adults at parents' evening.*		
School work and study skills		Progress in school —planning.*	Choices —strengths and potentials.**	Follow-up discussion.*	Making subject choices next year: visitors.**	
Academic guidance and careers education						How will you approach third-year decisions?**
Health and hygiene						
Personal interests					Summer holidays. What will you do? Planning.*	Personal statements.**

STAGE 31   *Summer Term*

(*First stage after half-term break*.)

PROGRAMME

Greetings.

Caring:
  Is everybody in good shape for the final half-term
  of year two?

Assembly:
  (a) Settle the form of the assembly.
  (b) Rehearse assembly.

Parents' evening:
  Alternative plans to be worked out in small
  groups with some open exchanges. Proposals to
  be formulated in readiness for submission to a
  formal meeting of the whole group in Stage 32.
  Confirm the date and the invitation to parents.

Authority and responsibility in our community:
  Discussion in small groups with open exchanges.
  Who carries responsibility and authority in our
  community? What are our personal responsibilities? Work through **Working Paper 21** in
  preparation for receiving a visitor in Stage 32.
  What issues do we to raise with our visitor?

OBJECTIVES AND COMMENTS

New momentum required to initiate the final half-
term of the second year.

Complete this as quickly as possible. Some individual rehearsal (supported by a small group) may
be possible outside pastoral time.

In Stage 32 a new, rather more formal style of
decision taking is to be introduced. This session
should crystallize clear proposals that will be put
forward in Stage 32 for formal discussion. This is
allied to an interest in the proceedings of public
bodies. For suggestions about the form of the
parents' evening, see **Working Paper 17**.

The purpose of these two sessions is to build on the
previous interest in other people in the
community, and to look at the inter-dependence
of public decision taking, the giving and taking of
instructions, and the general exercise of authority
and responsibility. Your visitor for Stage 32
needs a broad view of public affairs. Look
through **Working Paper 21** carefully, so that you
can choose points of emphasis that fit the general
interests and stage of development of the group.

STAGE 32

Summer Term

PROGRAMME

Greetings and caring.

Authority and responsibility in our community:
Receiving a visitor.
  - (a) Revise agenda for conversation with visitor:
    - personal interest in the visitor;
    - issues to be raised.
  - (b) Role-play reception and conclusion.

Meet the visitor.

  - (a) What did we learn?
  - (b) How well did we cope?

Parents' evening – formal group meeting:
  - (a) Small groups – to consider the formal proposals to be made to the full meeting. What is the small group's reaction to the proposals? Proposers and seconders to prepare their statements.
  - (b) Formal meeting. Proposals to be made and seconded, and then debated. Decisions through a concensus or by vote.
  - (c) For suggestions about the programme, see **Working Paper 17**.

Progress in school work;
Stocktaking, and the influence of school work on our future. Small group discussion with open exchanges.

  - (a) By this time next year you will have taken some important decisions about the courses and subjects you will follow for the rest of your school life – what kind of considerations will influence your choice of subjects?
  - (b) Report on e.g., the things that interest us; the subjects that we are good at; the kinds of careers that we might take up.
  - (c) As we get older, our ideas may change about the kind of careers we might follow. So how can we keep our choices open?
  - (d) Look forward to Stage 33 – stocktaking; and Stage 34 – some discussion with people who can tell us something about the decisions we face.

OBJECTIVES AND COMMENTS

Brief the visitor carefully, especially if he/she is accustomed to making speeches – a conversation is required. You will be wanting to help the young people begin to understand:

  - (a) the kinds of responsibility carried by members of the community;
  - (b) the nature of authority in community affairs;
  - (c) the inter-dependence of persons in authority and those whom they serve or direct;
  - (d) the young people's own responsibility in all this.

This is an event that will build on the skills of planning frameworks for statements, and of making public statements. It also links with 'Authority and responsibility in our community', and an introduction to the formal style of public bodies. The debate will be conducted in a fairly formal manner, with a proposer and seconder of any proposition, leading to a wider debate and decision. Probably it is a good idea to require each speaker to stand. The tutor will need to preside as chairman, and to help the proceedings along in an explanatory way. There may be links with receiving a visitor about authority, and responsibility.

At this stage you will be wanting to loosen up the discussion, and convey the importance to young people of keeping their options open.

Look forward to Stages 33 and 34, when more detailed discussions will take place.

Early arrangements will need to be made about visitors for Stage 35, who have had experience of the choices to be made. It would be possible to invite present third year pupils, but if so they may require considerable preparation.

STAGE 33

PROGRAMME

Greetings and caring.

Parents' evening:
  (a) Finalise decisions about the form of the event.
  (b) Plan what needs to be done and allocate jobs – small groups to take on specific functions such as:
    – planning part of the event;
    – preparing some publicity material;
    – planning reception.

Responsibility in the community – enquiry with parents. Work through small groups and open exchanges.

  (a) First throw up the main headings.
  (b) Next allocate headings to the small groups for them to suggest suitable prompts.
  (c) Create a small editing group to settle the form of enquiry. (Example in **Working Paper 20.**)
  (d) Role-play the approaches, and contract to complete the enquiry by a fixed day.

Progress in school and keeping options open:
  (a) Form small support groups who will help one another to explore their own positions, and to plan strategies for action.
  (b) Work through **Working Paper 31**, giving special attention to the personal action required.

OBJECTIVES AND COMMENTS

Suggestions for a parents' evenings will be found in **Working Paper 17**. Young people should conduct as much of the programme as possible, but the tutor will need to judge what to take on personally, or share with one or two young people. It is important that the young people have a successful experience.

The kind of enquiry that would be possible is illustrated by **Working Paper 20**.
Some young people will find it challenging to approach their parents in this way, and will need close preparation and support. Some may decide on joint action in approaching their parents.

Each young person will need a copy of **Working Paper 31**. The tutor will need an opportunity to see each young person's statement, both to support him/her in his efforts to improve his situation, and to take on any consultation that would be too delicate for the young person to initiate.

STAGE 34

Summer Term

PROGRAMME

Greetings and caring.

Enquiry with parents:
- (a) Report the experience. Role-play as appropriate.
- (b) Discussion in small groups and open exchanges. What did we learn from our parents about:

  - (i) what they saw as responsible behaviour by young people?
  - (ii) the influence that they thought that parents had on this?

- (c) How has the enquiry influenced what we would like to discuss at the parents' evening?

Parents' evening:
- (a) Revise the programme.
- (b) Progress report from the groups making preparations. Rehearsal of the part to be played by those who are to lead parts of the programme.
- (c) Reports about acceptance of invitations.
- (d) Receiving the parents as visitors to the school. Role-play reception, first as a demonstration, and then in small groups.

The parents' evening is to take place late in Stage 34 or early in Stage 35.

Progress in school:
- (a) The small support groups should consider the action required of each member, as indicated when completing **Working Paper 31.**

  - (i) Hear a progress report of action already taken. Help each member to plan immediate action for the next phase.
  - (ii) Open exchanges about matters of more general interest.

- (b) Look forward to visitor(s) in Stage 35. What matters do we want to raise?

OBJECTIVES AND COMMENTS

If some young people have not managed to conduct the enquiry with their parents, some additional support could be offered to enable them to see it through.

The experience arising from the enquiry is closely connected with the parents' evening.

Some strong feelings about relationships with parents may arise from this experience. Try to find time for some reflective discussion in small groups.

Some open exchanges may also be appropriate. The young people will need to consider their own contribution to creative relationships in the family (see also Stage 36).

Close planning and rehearsal required in order to ensure a successful experience by those taking part. Rehearsal may need to take place in sub-groups in order to cover sufficient ground in the time available. The tutor will need to offer *active* support at the actual event.

The tutor can offer only limited individual help to so many young people. The emphasis must be on self-help, with the close support of the small academic support group.

Significant help might be offered across the class by those who excel in certain subjects to others who find them difficult.

Open exchanges about general difficulties may help the tutor spot the points at which his/her own intervention is necessary.

STAGE 35

PROGRAMME

Greetings and caring.

Parents' evening:
Final preparation if the event has not yet taken place.
Review after the event – small groups and open exchanges.

(a) What were the main messages coming out of the discussions?
(b) Did these indicate the need for individual action by us?
(c) How well did we cope in receiving parents?
(d) How well did our members perform in introducing the programme? Is extra practice required?
(e) Was it a suitable programme for parents – how well did they cope?
(f) Has the whole exercise (including the enquiry) led to any new exchanges at home?
(g) Has it pointed to the need for any special personal action on our part?

Keeping options open:
Prepare to receive visitors.

(a) Revise agendas, not forgetting an interest in the visitor as a person
(b) Who will receive and who will conclude? Role-play this.

Meet the visitors.
(a) What did we learn?
(b) What are the lessons
– for immediate action?
– for our third year school work?
(c) How well did we cope with the visitors?

Summer activities:
What will you be doing with your summer holidays? Make preparation for some short individual statements in Stage 36.

OBJECTIVES AND COMMENTS

There is a great deal of potential personal experience in this event. Good preparation and support will help individual young people to practise skills fairly deliberately. And this level of personal consciousness will help them review the way in which they coped with the event. Supportive criticism should be quite acceptable at this stage.

The discussion about how the parents found the event, and any impact on exchanges at home, will be a good preparation for the discussion about the young people in their families in Stage 36. Look forward to the agenda for that discussion as part of your preparation for this review.

It is important that the group should seize the opportunity of discussing, with their visitors, what they face in the third year as a time of decision. Make sure that note-taking is continuing.

The exchanges should reinforce the function of the small support groups, and time should be given, in those small groups, to studying the implications of the exchanges with the visitors. Even the more timid members of the class should by now be playing their part quite readily in coping with visitors.

Three main objectives are:
to stimulate creative use of summer holidays; to encourage support of small groups in this; to reinforce skills in working out frameworks, and in making public statements.

STAGE 36

Summer Term

(Final stage of second year)

PROGRAMME

Greetings.

A review of the organisation of caring and administration with next term's arrangements in mind.

Keeping options open:
- (a) Review, in small groups, of action taken and required immediately.
- (b) Open exchanges about matters of general interest, and to inform one another about progress.
- (c) Summary – some of the factors that will influence decisions in the third year – discussions in small groups and open exchanges.
    - (i) e.g. The general kind of work to be undertaken as a career (although keep wide choices open).
    - (ii) The strengths and weakness of subjects.
    - (iii) Our ability to improve shaky subjects during the third year.

Family:
Small group discussion and open exchanges. Possible agenda:

- (a) As we grow older, how does this influence our relationships with our parents? For example, what happens about things that we want to do that parents find difficult to accept?
- (b) May this perhaps involve our parents also in a difficult adjustment?
- (c) Could we ease this situation by discussing differences reasonably, with as little heat as possible?

Role-play any situations which would help young people to practise new approaches.

Summer activities:
- (a) Small groups to revise the preparation and rehearsal of personal statements.
- (b) A number of individual statements about plans for the summer holidays, or about suitable interests.
- (c) Arrangements for any meetings to pursue activities together.

Farewells and good wishes.

OBJECTIVES AND COMMENTS

This needs to be carefully recorded, so that it can be revived at the beginning of the Autumn term.

A clear view of what is required may be as far as can be reached at this stage. Plans for action will need to be established early in the third year.

It is important to keep options open, both in the choice of subjects and of career.

Although the emphasis of the exchanges between parents and young people – including the enquiry – has been mainly about young people and their behaviour in the community, a good deal of attention will inevitably have been focused on the young person's relationships with parents. It is important that we capitalise on this, and encourage a reasonable and creative approach to this relationship by the young people.

An exchange of ideas could lead to positive action to support one another during the summer holidays in following some interesting activities. Neighbourhood groups could enrich their time together, and interest groups could travel to come together.

WORKING PAPERS FOR THE SECOND YEAR PROGRAMME

For use with
stage

Note

WORKING PAPER 16

Review of the group's behaviour

This framework should be used as the basis of small group discussion leading to open exchanges. It could represent a crucial point in settling in for second year pupils, who are adjusting to a new place in the school.

The emphasis is on a sense of responsibility. But if the exercise is to be seen as genuine to the young people, it will also need to be treated as an opportunity to check that their general school experience is creative and appropriate.

The exercise could lead to a continuing discussion over the next few stages.

1   How well do we know one another as a group?
    Do we tend to leave anybody out?

2   Are we good at cooperating with one another and supporting one another?

3   Are we reasonably good at cooperating with the teachers whom we meet?

4   Do we behave with consideration to the other people in the school, and are we helpful in particular to the younger pupils?

5   Are we orderly and courteous as we move around the school?

6   Are we dressed tidily?

7   Do we do our share in keeping the school clean and free of litter?

8   Is there anything to which we should give special attention?

WORKING PAPER 17

Second year parents' evening

It is suggested that the event should take the form of a dialogue between young people and parents, initiated largely by the young people. Since the numbers should not be too large, it would be advisable for each form to plan its own parents' evening.

Themes

The evening could serve as an opportunity to build upon a number of the themes followed during the second year, especially:
- (a) skills in meeting, greeting and conversing with adults;
- (b) skills in preparing and making public statements;
- (c) an interest in the lives of other people in our community;
- (d) the study of authority and responsibility in the community;
- (e) an interest in the part that the family plays in all this;
- (f) some attention paid to the responsibilities of young people.

The evening will have the additional purpose of fostering communication between parents and young people. For this reason, all working groups should consist of both adults and young people.

Programme

The programme should be led as far as possible by the young people, each leading possibly a single item, with the parents taking part. The programme might take the following form:

1   Greetings – handtaking – meeting by name as many people as possible.

2   Support – some kind of support exercise, preferably involving young people and adults together. A trust walk might be appropriate.

3   Conversations – getting to know one another. Brief conversations in pairs for a few minutes. Change pairs several times if there is time.

4   The lives and interests of people in our community:
    (a) Very brief public statements by two or three young people in turn,
        telling what impressed them about their experience in that study.
    (b) Discussion in small groups of parents and young people together, with
        open exchanges, based on the public statements, or on an agenda such
        as:
         (i) Are people in our community happy with their jobs?
        (ii) Is ours a stimulating community to live in?
       (iii) Are there sufficient opportunities for interest and recreation?
        (iv) Is there anything that we as individuals could do to improve the
             quality of life in our community?

5   Authority and responsibility in our community:
    (a) Very brief public statements by two or three young people arising out of
        their own discussion of this topic.
    (b) Small group discussion with open exchanges.
        Possible agenda:
         (i) Do we actually meet the people taking responsibility for the
             services and good order in our community?
        (ii) Is there enough cooperation between the people in authority and
             the other members of our community?
       (iii) How much individual responsibility do we each take for the
             general well-being of our community?

6   The family and the community:
    (a) Brief public statements by two or three young people.
    (b) Small group discussion and open exchanges.
         (i) What do we mean when we suggest that young people should play
             their part in the community in a responsible way?
        (ii) How can parents help in this respect?

Conclusion

    (a) One or two young people thank the parents for their help and interest.
    (b) Farewells – handtaking as a symbol of good wishes.

WORKING PAPER 18

What kind of friend am I?

1   Can my friends rely on me?
    (a) Am I there when I am needed, or when I said I would be there?
    (b) Can friends depend on my support when they are in difficulties?
    (c) Can friends trust me not to tell other people their secrets?

2   Am I prepared to stay with my friends even when they don't please me?

3   Am I really able to listen to my friends?
    (a) Can they tell me their troubles and know that I care?
    (b) Am I able to give them confidence to talk freely to me?

4   Do I confide in my friends? Do they know that I can trust them just as they can trust me?

WORKING PAPER 19

Conversations between girls and boys

A   Conversations in mixed small groups of, say, four pupils.

1   What kind of things make you laugh?

2   What kind of things make you sad?

3   What makes you really pleased?

4   What makes you angry?

5   What are the most important things in your life?

6   What do you have to do that you wish you could avoid?

7   Describe yourself as you imagine you will be in ten years' time.

8   Because I am a girl/boy I am expected to . . .

B   Each group should help one of their members to prepare a one-minute statement to the rest of the group about:

This is what I think it must feel like to be a boy/girl . . .

And this is why . . .

WORKING PAPER 20

Enquiry with parents – responsibility in the community

This is an example of the kind of enquiry that might be conducted by young people with their parents.

> We are looking at the responsibilities of young people in the community, and we should be very glad of your views about these questions.

1   What was there to do outside your home when you were my age?

2   How were you expected to behave?

3   How did young people behave when they were out with their friends?

4   How is it different today?

5   In what ways could young people today accept more responsibility?

6   Do parents influence this kind of thing?

7   Do parents experience any difficulty in influencing the behaviour of their children when they are out in the community?

8   Do you think there is enough contact between parents and their children?

9   As you know, my form is planning to hold a special evening with parents to discuss this kind of thing.
    (a) Will you be able to accept our invitation?
    (b) Should this topic form part of the programme?

WORKING PAPER 21

Authority and responsibility in our community

Work through small group discussion and open exchanges, using the framework below as an agenda.

1   Let us consider some of the people who have to take responsibility for keeping things going in our community.
    What kinds of things have to be looked after?
    The responses may include, for example –
        services to our homes;
        roads and the environment;
        services to people in need;
        health and hospital services;
        law and order – police and judiciary;
        clubs, societies and recreational facilities;
        schools and other educational facilities.

2   Take one of these areas (each small group should choose one of those put forward).
    What do you feel that the people responsible for the kind of service that you have chosen
    (a) have to do when organising their work?
    (b) have to do when facing the public – both serving us and justifying their actions?

3   In order for our community to be running smoothly, someone must give instructions about what we must do.
    (a) What instructions are given by the people responsible for the service that you are looking at?
    (b) Why do people follow these instructions, and do what is required of them?

4   What individual and personal responsibilities do we have within our community?

5   Preparing for a visitor – preparation of agenda:
    (a) Come to know the visitor as a person, and as a responsible citizen – what part does he/she play?
    (b) Prepare points for discussion about people exercising authority, and about our individual responsibility.

WORKING PAPER 22

Other people in our community – an action research programme

The following are some examples of the kind of enquiries that might be appropriate.

Occupation   (Do not forget that the mother of a young family may have that as her 'occupation'.)

What kind of work do you do?
What do you like most about your job?
What do you like least about your job?
Are you satisfied with your job, or would you rather be doing something else?

Home and District

Where do you live?
How would you describe your district?
What do you like about your district?
Is there anything you do not like about it?

Family

Are you married?
Have you any children?
Do you live near, or with your parents, brothers and sisters?
What do you find most rewarding about your family life?
What do you find most difficult about your family life?

Interests

What do you choose for relaxation?
Have you any interests or hobbies?
Are there suitable opportunities to follow your interests?
Are there any other interests that you would like to follow?

Life in General

What, for you, are the most important things in life?
What are the least enjoyable things in life?
What kind of things give you the greatest pleasure?

Conclusion

We are interested in the people in our community. Is there anything else that I should be asking you?
Thank you for your help.

WORKING PAPER 23

The roles we play

There is only one 'me', but I may find myself behaving differently in one situation from another.

Work in small mixed groups of boys and girls, using the working paper as an agenda for discussion. Small group discussion should lead to open exchanges.

Section one – a number of roles in life

1   What do we mean when we say that we are a son or daughter?
   (a) Are we expected to behave in certain ways towards our parents?
   (b) Do we expect our parents to behave in certain ways towards us?
   (c) What happens if we do not behave in the way that is expected of us? Can you think of a recent example?
   (d) Show us what happened (in role-play).

2   *Brother and Sister*
   (a) Are we expected to behave in certain ways to our brothers and sisters?
   (b) Show us how you would normally behave (in role-play).
   (c) What is the difference between being a son and a brother, or a daughter and a sister?

3   *Pupil*
   (a) What is expected of us as pupils?
   (b) What do we expect of our teachers?
   (c) How do we know that we are not doing what is expected of us
      (i) by the teacher?
      (ii) by our classmates?
   (d) Do we all behave exactly the same way as pupils?
      Think of some of the people in our class – do they behave differently from one another?
      (Show this in role-play if appropriate.)
   (e) Do we expect our class members to behave in these different ways? Do we sometimes keep them up to it? So is the way we behave in class a combination of what is expected of us and our own special inclinations?
      Is this also true at home?

4 *With friends*
   (a) Are we expected to behave in certain ways to our friends?
   (b) Do we behave in the same way with each of our friends?
        If not, what makes the difference?
   (c) Does each of our friends have his own individual way of behaving
        when he is with us?

5 *With the people we play with*
   (a) Are certain things expected of us when we are playing games?
   (b) What would make the people we play with angry with us?

6 *Our Several Roles*
   (a) So do we behave differently as a son and daughter, as brother or sister,
        as pupil, as friend, or when playing?
   (b) Do we have other roles in life?

7 Do we have our own way of playing a number of these roles?

Section two – gender roles

1 At home – what is expected of a son and not of a daughter, and vice-versa?

2 What is expected of a brother and not of a sister, and vice-versa?

3 Venturing outside the home – what is expected by parents of a boy and not
   of a girl, and vice-versa?

4 Why are there these differences of expectation between boys and girls?

5 In school are there differences in what is expected of boys and of girls?

6 Amongst friends, are there any differences between what is expected from
   boys and girls?

7 At play, what are the differences in expectations?

8 Do we become what we are because of us, or because of what is expected
   of us?

9   Do you feel that all the expectations are helpful?

10   How do you think boys should behave towards girls, and girls should behave towards boys?

WORKING PAPER 24

Communications workshop

This working paper is intended to help groups explore areas of communication other than the kind of verbal exchanges well represented by many of the other exercises. It should be used as an agenda in the hands of the tutor conducting the session. Although much of the activity is conducted through small groups, direction from the centre will serve to move on the action at the pace that seems most appropriate.

Exchanges between the groups about their experience and feelings should be a continuing part of the exercise. There are many points at which the members of the group could be encouraged to be inventive and to take the activity beyond the prompts offered below.

There is enough material here for several short sessions, dependent upon the climate created and the sensitivity with which the exercises are practised.

Section one

1   *Greetings, Support and Contracts*
    Greet and take the hand of a number of members of the group, and renew contracts of support in the exploratory session to follow.

2   *Hands*
    (a) Find a partner.
        Take the hand of your partner.
        Take both hands of your partner.
        Explore the hands of your partner with your eyes closed.
        Now explore your own hands.
        Explore your partner's hands again.
        Is there much difference in the feel of the hands?
        Now take your partner's hand again – what do you feel that he/she is saying by the way he/she takes your hands?
        Compare your experience with that of a neighbouring pair.
    (b) Change partners – preferably in mixed pairs.
        Repeat the exercise.
        Is there a difference between the hands of the two partners that you have had?
        Do they seem to be saying something different to you by the way they take your hand?

N.B. If you break the programme at any stage and recommence later, it is important to warm up again before moving into the later exercises. Handtaking and renewing contracts of support in the exercise may be a suitable warm-up.

(c) Change partners.
Repeat the exercise and the questions.
Now, with the same partner, see whether you can express ideas through the way you take hands. For example, without speaking, take hands and say:
'I am very pleased to see you.'
(First one try it and then the other.)
Now try:
'Congratulations. Well done!'
'I don't like doing this really.'
'You're all right – I'll look after you.'
'You rather frighten me.'
'I know I can trust you and I'm really relying on you.'
Now each one in turn tries to express some idea through your hands, and the other tries to understand what is intended.

3 *Pressure on Forearm*
Change partners.
Take hands.
Take both hands.
Explore your partner's hands.
Now, without speaking, through a little pressure on your partner's forearm, say:
'Hello, pleased to see you.'
Now the other partner try it. Did you convey that message? Try some more messages.
'Come on, cheer up, shake yourself out of it.'
'You're all right!' Reassure your partner with great gentleness.
'Yes, I know you are sad. I'm here to share it with you.'
Now invent a few messages of your own, and try to discuss your partner's message.

4 *Hands on both Shoulders*
Try to express:
'So there you are – I've been looking for you.'
'It's good to see you – haven't seen you for a long time.'
'Oh, go on with you – it is not as bad as that!'
Can you express anything else in this way?

Are there things that it is difficult to express through hands on shoulders?
Compare it with pressure on a forearm.

5   *Shoulder to Shoulder*
    Try to express:
        'Hello, how are you?'
        'Go on, get on with it.'
    What else can you express in this way?

6   *Posture – the Whole Body*
    Work in small groups. Sitting or standing as appropriate, one person at a
    time will try to portray the following:
        relaxed and cheerful;
        defiant;
        sulky;
        keen and alert;
        bored;
        afraid.
    Try other postures, and the rest of your small group will try to read the
    message.

7   *Shadowing*
    In partnership, one partner leads with hand movements. The other follows
    with his/her own hands as if the two partners' hands were held together with
    an elastic band. First one leads and then the other.
    The purpose is to help your partner to follow you, not to defeat him/her.
        How considerate are you of the person who is following you?
        How sensitive are you to the other person's movements and intentions?

Section two

This is supplementary material that will build upon the exercises practised in
stage one. Before beginning each section, it is advisable to recall the
appropriate earlier experience by a brief repetition of some of the previous
material.

Hands
Find a partner. Warm up by repeating the first exercise in Stage One. Encourage
an extension of the free expression through hands as outlined in 2 (c).

Now, in turn, respond to one another and gradually develop a 'conversation' through hand pressures. Check with your partner your own understanding of what is being expressed.

Turn, with your partner, to another pair.
Share their hand conversation, and they will also learn about yours.

How much can you express through hand pressures, and what are the limitations?
  Small group discussion and open exchanges.

Hand Gestures
In small groups see how many different ways you can gesture with your hands – and without words – 'Come over here.'
What feelings or message is conveyed in each case?
What else can you 'say' through hand gestures?

Shadowing
Find a partner. Warm up by repeating some of the exercises in 7 above.
Now change the leadership from partner to partner, so that it is difficult to see who is leading.
Next take the leadership backwards and forwards in a kind of 'conversation'.
Can you express any ideas, questions and answers through this conversation?

Mime
Working in small groups, take turns to mime some simple activities,
e.g. brushing your hair;
      putting on a coat;
      washing up;
      cutting and buttering bread;
      stroking a cat;
      comforting a little boy or girl.

Now invent some mimes of your own, and the other members of your group must guess what you are portraying.

Next portray feelings or moods,
e.g. cheerful, sad, uncertain, frightened, relieved.
      Do you *feel* these moods, or are you only acting them?
      Try again and really feel them.

Now invent your own expressions and the other members of your group will try to get the message. Some of these may be a recall of your recent feelings or experience.

Two people together, with the other members of your small group looking on and sharing the discussion, mime a series of scenes,
e.g. being told what to do and not wanting to do it;
       one is sad and the other is consoling;
       you want to get up and go – your partner does not want to bother.

Now invent your own scenes – or recall something involving feelings and emotions that has happened to you recently. Some of these may involve the whole of your small group.

The Tone of Speech
The *way* in which something is said sometimes carries a stronger message than the words themselves. Try this for yourself in small groups. Try saying something quite simple – e.g. 'So you're here, Harry' – in ways that would denote:

surprise,	pleasure,	disappointment,
anger,	boredom,	encouragement.

Try longer speeches in, say, a supportive style or a mocking way. Go on inventing new situations in new tones of expression.

What hidden messages of this kind do you hear in the speech of people you normally meet?

How do you operate – what messages do you send through the tone of your expression?

WORKING PAPER 25

Empathy exercise

A Shadowing – Sensitivity towards a partner

1 Warm up by one following the movement of the other as practised in Stage 16 (Working Paper 24, Section One, 7, and Section Two).

2 Change the leadership from one partner to the other.

3 General discussion:
   (a) How sensitive are we to what our partner is doing or about to do?
   (b) How considerate are we in leading our partner?

4 Each partner engages in leading the other to express a mood, e.g.

agitated	– relaxed;	pleased	– angry;
friendly	– hostile;	encouraging	– discouraging;
confident	– timid;	unhappy	– happy.

   What other moods can you suggest?

   Break off at fairly frequent intervals, so that the partners can discuss their progress, and there can be some open exchanges and demonstrations.

B Conversations in twos, and introductions in fours

1 Personal conversations between partners (what it is like to be me) stimulated by an agenda called, step by step, by the tutor.
   e.g. (a) The things that I enjoy the most are . . .
       (b) The things that I dislike the most are . . .
       (c) The things that I fear most are . . .
       (d) The things that I find easiest are . . .
       (e) The things that I find most difficult are . . .
       (f) With older people I . . .
       (g) With strangers of my own age I . . .
       (h) With my friends I . . .

(i) |When I have to talk with a boy/girl I . . .
(j) I think other people see me as . . .
(k) I wish I could . . .
(l) Most people don't realise that I . . .
(m) I think it is very important that we should . . .

2   Each pair joins another pair. Each must introduce his or her partner to the other pair *in the first person*.

How good are we at putting ourselves in our partner's shoes, and speaking as if we were that person? And how well have we listened?

WORKING PAPER 26

Spontaneity workshop
Being imaginative and inventive

This programme is about taking normal objects and activities into the realm of novelty and fantasy. It is suggested that small groups should each take a topic, and should be encouraged to be as inventive as possible. A fairly brief time limit should be set, and each small group should report its topic and its findings to the whole group.

There are enough suggestions below for a number of occasions, especially if a number of groups work simultaneously on the same topic. This is the kind of activity that could be fitted into an odd ten minutes, once the group has developed a 'feel' for what is possible. The suggestion of further topics could be made part of the exercise.

The exercise represents a kind of brainstorming, to help with the rapid production and exchange of ideas, in keeping with the skills of producing ideas for agendas and frameworks. There is also an affinity with empathy: the ability to take a new position, slightly outside our own frame of reference.

Work in small groups, who will report their findings to the whole group.
1   Describe a school that is about:
    (a) becoming a good fish;
    (b) being a clever gnome;
    (c) becoming a pretty cloud;
    (d) being a good tortoise.

2   You are living in a world without ground and floors.
    (a) Describe your classroom.
    (b) Tell about what you are learning.

3   Think of as many ways of using an orange as you can. Make it any size you like. For example, could you live in it? How?

4   The people in the classroom are the furniture, and the furniture the people. Describe what is happening.

5   What can you do with five live matches? They can be any size you like.

6   The things in the classroom have taken root and are growing. Describe what happens.

7   Invent something that will do your homework.

8   A man from Mars has just been a visitor to the group. Describe what happened and the conversation you had with him.

WORKING PAPER 27

Homework – programme and planning

Name .... Form ....

The purpose of this enquiry is to help you to think about the way you plan and approach your homework, and to help your teachers to understand any difficulties that you may face. It is important that you should be honest with yourself in completing the enquiry.

1 Timetable
   Note the exact time that you begin and finish each piece of homework through a single week. If you do it in bits, note the start and finish of each period of time given to it. The table on the next page will help you.

2 Approach
   (a) How easily do you get down to your homework?
        For example, do you get straight into it, do you dither, or does it vary?
        Try to describe your approach.

   (b) Does your homework tend to hang over your head for most of the evening?

   (c) How do you feel when you have finished?

3 Where do you usually do your homework?
   (a) Is the room usually occupied by other people also?
        How many people?

   (b) Is a television set usually within your vision?

   (c) Is a radio, television set, or amplifier usually within your hearing? With what kind of programmes?

4 Are you sometimes very anxious about your homework? What about?

5 Have you shared this enquiry with your parents?

Timetable   A week's homework

Day	Subject	Time		*How easy or difficult?					*Did you enjoy it?				
		started	finished	very easy	fairly easy	all right	fairly difficult	very difficult	very much	a little	all right	no	not at all

* Tick appropriate column.

WORKING PAPER 28

How do we find school?

This paper is intended as a framework for discussion in small groups with open exchanges.

1   *Relationships with other pupils*:
    (a) Is school a friendly place?
    (b) Do you have enough friends around you in school?
    (c) How do you get on with the older pupils in the school?
    (d) And how do you get on with the younger children?

2   *Relationships with staff*:
    (a) Do you feel that you know your teachers well enough and that they know you?
    (b) Do you feel that you can approach a teacher when you are wanting any information or help?
    (c) How do you see the senior staff?
    (d) What part do you play in the kind of relationships you have with the staff in the school? Would it be possible for you to help your own position?

3   *School work*:
    The purpose of school is to help you to learn.
    (a) Do you feel that the amount or kind of work is demanding enough?
    (b) Do you feel that you are sufficiently helped to understand?
    (c) Have you ideas about the range of subjects you are taught?

4   *The school*:
    (a) Is the school something that you can feel proud to belong to?
    (b) Do you feel that its image could be improved in any way?

5   *The school and your parents*:
    (a) How is the school seen by your parents?
    (b) Do we do enough to gain the interest and cooperation of parents? What more would you suggest?

WORKING PAPER 29

Progress with school work – Fourth self-assessment

Name .... Form ....

1   I feel that I am making satisfactory progress with the following subjects:

2   I feel that I am doing especially well with . . .

3   I feel that I am falling behind with . . .

4   I feel that, with a little more effort, I could do better at . . .

5   In spite of making some effort, I do not seem to be able to make much progress with . . .

6   I have difficulty with homework in . . .

7   I find it fairly easy to do my homework in . . .

8   The greatest difficulty I have with homework is to . . .

9   I feel that in general, my approach to organising my homework is . . .

Summary and Objectives:

1   I should be glad of some extra help with . . .

2   I feel that I should
    (a) consult .... about ....
    (b) consult .... about ....

3   I must make a special effort with . . .

WORKING PAPER 30

Progress with school work – Fifth self-assessment

Name .... Form ....

Part I   Progress in subjects

1   This term I have been coping quite satisfactorily with . . .

2   I feel that I have improved at . . .

3   I am having some difficulty with . . .

4   And I do not seem at all able to cope with . . .

Part II   Some general skills

5   How confident are you in your approach to school work – are you prepared to 'have a go'?

6   Does the level of interest in what you do vary from subject to subject? Which subjects?

High level of interest   Moderate level   Low level

How closely is this connected with the effort you have made in those subjects?

7   Can you 'attack' your work – really go at it?
    Or do you dither?

8   Are there any general skills that could be improved? For example:

    (a) Drawing diagrams, maps and illustrations?

    (b) Getting to the basic ideas behind what you are being asked?

    (c) Reasoning things out? What kind of things?

    (d) Doing calculations?

    (e) Anything else?

Part III   Summary and action

1   I feel that I must make a special effort with the following subjects . . .

2   These are the general study skills that I need to give special attention to . . .

3   I feel that I need some special help with the following . . .

WORKING PAPER 31

Name .... Form ....

Keeping options open

By this time next year, you will have taken some important decisions about your future courses and subjects. At this stage you will want to keep your options open, and maintain a wide range of subjects at a reasonable level.

This is an opportunity for some stocktaking about your progress in the subjects you are taking. As you work through this enquiry, share your thinking with a small support group of classmates, so that you can help one another in your attempts to improve your situation.

1   I feel confident about a number of subjects, especially . . .

2   Some subjects are less secure, but with a special effort I should be able to reach a satisfactory level. This would apply to . . .

3   (a) I am having greater difficulty with . . .

    (b) Of these subjects, I would especially like to improve in . . .

4   What are the reasons for your difficulties?
    (a) For example, are they about,
         (i) understanding the material?

         (ii) putting ideas together?

         (iii) a lack of effort rather than a lack of ability?

    (b) Or are you having difficulties with some more general study skills that affect several subjects, such as
         – memorising material?
         – writing things up?
         – quickness with figures?
         – speed of writing?
         – poor spelling?

– reading easily, and understanding what you read?
– laying out outlines and frameworks?
– seeing the general principles involved in solving problems?
– applying principles to problem solving?
Underline any that are especially difficult for you.

(c) Consider the subjects with which you have difficulties:

in . . . . my main difficulties are . . .

In . . . . my main difficulties are . . .

In . . . . my main difficulties are . . .

5   Now consider – in consultation with your small support group – to whom
you might turn for help.

With . . . . I might get help from/by . . .

With . . . . I might get help from/by . . .

With . . . . I might get help from/by . . .

6   Action:
This is the action I need to take:

(a)

(b)

(c)

Appendix

Evaluation – The Progress of Individual Young People

The Schedule

This evaluation schedule should be seen as an opportunity to review the development of the group members' social skills, their self-feelings and their attitudes to school. The schedule is designed to provide opportunities for an examination of individual progress, and to note even small movements in the many facets of life.

Most of the headings lead to a *continuum* from one extreme to another. Typical descriptions are given of the two extremes and a central point, but judgment should be made within the general spirit of the themes rather than being tied to the specific descriptions. Placing along any line will be a matter of some subtlety, so intermediate positions will be needed on many of the *continua*.

Original Position

It is important that there should be an early statement of the member's position as the work begins. It may be possible to seek the advice of other people who have been regularly in touch with the person concerned so that their views can be taken into account when determining the member's original positions on the continua.

However, it has been our experience that it is difficult for the outside observer to penetrate sufficiently deeply into the individual's personal position to be able to offer a really sensitive judgment. So it is therefore possible that some retrospective adjustment to the original placing may be needed as the on-going discussion involved in the work reveals the true original position.

The Group Member's Self-Assessment

Perhaps the most reliable guide available to us is the group member's own assessment as he becomes increasingly articulate about his own personal position and feels himself encouraged by a supportive group. It is also an important part of the group member's experience to evaluate his own position and progress. For this reason this evaluation paper should be used deliberately and creatively as part of the experience.

The specific sections of the schedule could be dealt with step-by-step as the emphasis of the programme touches the issues raised by each part of the schedule.

Evaluation Schedule

Meeting and Greeting People

| Shy/abrupt. Avoiding if possible. Embarrassed by approaches. Passes off. | Can respond with reasonable ease, as long as the other person makes a move. | Can make the running. Puts the other person at ease. Can negotiate in tricky situations. |

Known peers _____

Any comments:

Meeting and Greeting People

	Shy/abrupt. Avoiding if possible. Embarrassed by approaches. Passes off.	Can respond with reasonable ease, as long as the other person makes a move.	Can make the running. Puts the other person at ease. Can negotiate in tricky situations.
Strange peers			
	Any comments:		
Opposite sex			
	Any comments:		
Known adults			
	Any comments:		
Strange adults			
	Any comments:		

Eye Contact

	Acute embarrassment. Always looks down or away.	Can manage momentary eye contact, but tends to avoid.	Easy and unconcerned.
	Any comments:		

Conversation

Fluency	Abrupt. Monosyllabic.	Operates through brief bursts. Can respond to the other person's prompting	Sustained conversation.
	Comments:		
Depth	Narrow. Concrete.	Can describe events and interests.	Wide. Personal. Abstract.
	Comments:		

Listening

| Intolerant of the other's statement. Full of his own statement/of himself. | Tolerates the other person's statement. Will usually stay with him long enough to hear him out. | Deep and encouraging interest in the other person. |

Comments:

Speaking in Public (e.g. the classroom)

| Will avoid if possible. Embarrassed/ confused if required to respond in public | Can respond without embarrassment, but rarely takes the initiative. | Can make a balanced and sensitive contribution in public without embarrassment. |

Comments:

Persistence/Consistency

| Fickle and changeable. Gives up when slightest effort required. Cannot give attention for many minutes. | Will attempt a task, but interest wanes after some time. | Sticks to even a difficult undertaking, in an effort to see it through. |

Comments:

Resilience to Uncertainty

| Cannot stand uncertainty. Contracts out or causes trouble. | Uneasy with uncertainty, but can be contained. | Copes easily and without anxiety with uncertainty. |

Comments:

Resilience to Opposition and Hostility

Meets opposition or hostility with immediate anger or submission.	Meets like with like. Escapes rather than copes.	Is not easily embarrassed or stirred up by hostility. Meets hostility with reasoned response.

Comments:

Coping with Obstacles

Immediately frustrated, angry, defeated.	Persists to a point, and then becomes frustrated.	Looks around the problem and considers alternatives. Can relax when progress is not possible.

Comments:

Response to Authority

Confused, submissive, rebellious, angry.	Tends to respond strongly to authority- sometimes unreasonably. Easily cowed by authority behaviour.	Engages with ease. Copes with even unreasonable authority behaviour.

Comments:

Self-confidence

Timid. Very easily deterred from action requiring any personal risk.	Needs encouragement and support in engaging in any action that involves new people or situations.	Will take on challenging situations without stress.

Comments:

Self-esteem

| Strong self-doubts. Sense of being a failure. Sense of being unworthy. | Unsure of his own value, but not unduly inhibited by it. | Relaxed in accepting other people's regard. |

Comments:

Attitude to School Work

| Antagonistic, apathetic, resistant, passive. | Works as required without giving much trouble. | Cooperative, enthusiastic, consistent effort. |

Comments:

Attendance at School

| Frequent unjustified absences. | Attends regularly, but absents himself whenever reasonable excuse offers itself. | Faultless in regular attendance and on time. |

Comments:

Index